The Light in the Lantern

True Stories for Your Faith Journey

James L. Henderschedt

Resource Publications, Inc.
San Jose, California

Editorial director: Kenneth Guentert
Managing editor: Kathi Drolet
Production: Elizabeth J. Asborno
Illustrator: Sharon K. Hanley

Reprint Department
Resource Publications, Inc.
160 E. Virginia Street, Suite 290
San Jose, CA 95112-5848

Library of Congress Cataloging in Publication Data
The light in the lantern : true stories for your faith journey / James L. Henderschedt.
p. cm.
Includes index.
1. Christian fiction, American. I. Title.
PS3558.E4797L54 1991
813'.54—dc20 91-33639
CIP

5 4 3 2 1 | 95 94 93 92 91

To Betty, John, Beth, and Tom
for your love, encouragement, and inspiration.

Contents

Preface

"Are your stories true?"

This is the most-often-asked question after a workshop or "storytelling concert." I have had it asked of me by children and adults alike. It is a question that I have learned to take very seriously and answer honestly.

Are my stories true? Yes, they most certainly are—every one of them. What makes them true is not that they are made up of facts that can be indisputably proven. Nor are they true because they can be checked and cross-referenced by teams of scholars. They are true because they are created out of the depth of my own spiritual pondering and faith journey. Each story in this book was shaped out of the raw material of faith, designed on the drawing board of meditation, and forged on the anvil of experience. There is more than a piece of me in this collection of short stories. And they are true because they are my stories.

These stories will also become true for you when you take them as your own and make them a part of your life and meditation process. Although they can entertain, their main purpose for being is to invite you to stop at the way-side inns along the road of your own faith journey and take the time to ponder the mysteries of God and his Kingdom. We are akin when you and I are united on some quest to discover what we believe. When you read "Dennis Meets St. Peter," it is my prayer that you will examine your concept of heaven and hell. I hope that "You Want It Made out of What?" challenges you to wonder when you might have made a god out of the gift instead of the Giver. I would want to be with you when you look into "The Light in the Lantern" to share what you see.

If these stories are used in a small group setting, I do hope that the stories can be true for the community. How does "Can This Be Home?" reflect or challenge how the group meets and treats the "exiles" in its midst? After reading "The Night They Were There," the group members could be wondering about those whom they would be most comfortable eating with—and those with whom they would be most uncomfortable. And, if your small group is like those I have had association with, there will be plenty of those who go through life thinking that they're a "just-a" (just a housewife, just a mechanic, just a laborer, just a mother, etc.) who may get a different view of their self worth and their place in God's whole scheme of things after reading and discussing "Among the Pots and Pans."

Each story is a challenge in itself to look closely at our own life and experience: to laugh and cry, to sing and shout, to pray and meditate, to speak and keep silent. These stories are true because they are truly my stories. These stories are true because they are truly your stories.

I pray that my story and your story will come together in God's story, and that where they meet will be the path to enlightenment where we will be able to hear with more than our ears and see with more than our eyes, as did the disciples in "What the Disciples Heard."

So, dear pilgrim, welcome once again to the journey. I will look forward to meeting you at the Inn of Contemplation and sharing with you the nourishing food and drink of the Spirit. May your journey be safe, exciting, and wonder-full.

Jim Henderschedt

Acknowledgments

The following stories were previously published with a one-time publishing agreement with *Celebration: An Ecumenical Worship Resource*, published by The National Catholic Publishing Co., 115 East Armour Boulevard, Kansas City, Missouri, 64111-1295:

"Held in the Arms of Grace," vol. 18, no. 1 (January 1989): 12-13; "Grandma Richardson' s Treasure," vol. 18, no. 8 (August 1989): 306-307; "Reruns," vol. 18, no. 2 (February 1989): 56-57; "The Light in the Lantern," vol. 19, no. 6 (June 1990): 226-227; "Sal's Tavern," vol. 18, no. 9 (September 1989): 350-351; What the Disciples Heard," vol. 19, no. 7 (July 1990): 270-271; "Can This Be Home?" vol. 19, no. 2 (February 1990): 57-58; "The Night *They* Were There," vol. 19, no. 9 (September 1990): 354-355; "Among the Pots and Pans," vol. 19, no. 10 (October 1990): 398-399; "Stuart's Hearing," vol. 18, no. 10 (October 1990): 390-391; "Her Master's Voice," vol. 19, no. 5 (May 1990): 107-108; "The Truck Stop," vol. 18, no. 11 (November 1990): 432-433; "The Picnic," vol. 18, no. 5 (May 1989): 178-179; "What Is One to Do?" vol. 18, no. 7 (July 1989): 262-263; "The Solo," vol. 18, no. 6 (June 1989): 222-223; "One Cold and Windy Day," vol. 18, no. 11 (November 1989): 434-435.

"How the Christmas Star Got Its Light" was also published by *Celebration* (December 1990) as a special folder.

The Light in the Lantern

Held in the Arms of Grace

Theme: compassion; grace
Scripture: Luke 4:14-21
Season: Epiphany (3rd Sunday, C cycle)

"I'm so hot!"

"I know. It's the fever. Just lie back while I put this cloth on your forehead."

"Your hand feels so good on my cheek."

"You're crying."

"It has been so long since I have felt the touch of someone's hand. Everybody is afraid of me. The closest I come to being touched are the nurses and interns here at the hospital, and they always wear rubber gloves."

"People don't understand and they are always afraid of things they don't understand."

"But you're not wearing gloves."

"Well, let's just say that if there is a risk, there are some risks that need to be taken."

"You are very kind."

"It is nice of you to say so. I try to be. Sometimes kindness is misinterpreted. Some people do not recognize when others are following the whisperings of their heart."

"It's ironic, isn't it?"

"What is?"

"Well, you come to the hospital because you are sick and want to get well and you leave in worse condition than when you were admitted."

"Is that what happened to you?"

"Yes. I was having surgery. It was not really supposed to be very serious—not life-threatening anyway. During the operation I needed a blood transfusion. That was before anyone knew anything about AIDS. Blood wasn't tested as thoroughly in those days. Just one pint, that's all it took, and now here I am."

"Are you angry?"

"No...Yes!...I don't know. Who should I be angry at? It's just that there's so much I wanted to do. But I won't be able to do it. I'm dying. At least the doctors have been honest with me. It is just a matter of time, and I don't think there is much of that left anymore. I am so tired. My body is burning and yet I shiver with chills."

"It's the fever from the infection. Do you want more covers? Here, let me freshen that towel on your forehead."

"No, let it go. I'm okay. Just stay with me and talk to me."

"I'm here. I won't go away."

"I have a personal question. Do you mind?"

"No, not at all. What is it?"

"Are you married?"

"Yes, I am. I have a wonderful wife and two lovely children."

"Do you love your wife?"

"Very much."

"Does she love you?"

"Very much also."

"I always wanted to get married and have a couple children."

"You were never married?"

"No...almost, though. I was going with this guy. We were talking about getting engaged. But then this happened."

"Did you love him?"

"Yes, I did; in fact I still do in a strange way. I wanted to be his wife, the mother of his children. But things didn't work out that way. At first he told me he would be by my side all the way. But then the visits became fewer and fewer. I understand he married someone else last week."

"Is there anyone else?"

"No, I'm all alone...an only child and both parents are dead. I only have you."

"I'm very happy I can be here with you."

"Is it getting dark?"

"Is it getting dark for you?"

"Yes it is. Tell me the truth. Has the sun gone behind some clouds? Is it close to night?"

"No, it is not getting dark."

"Is this it? Is this how it is?"

"I don't know. What is it like?"

"I think I am going to be afraid."

"It's okay to be afraid."

"I don't even know your name."

"Just call me Josh."

"Josh? Joshua? I like that name. Josh, I would like to ask a favor of you, but I am afraid."

"Try asking it. It may not be as difficult as it seems."

"Would you...do you think your wife would mind...hold me?"

"I'm sure she would understand. Here, let me sit on the edge of the bed. There, how's that?"

"That's fine, thank you. Oh Josh, can you hear that?"

"What do you hear?"

"It's music, beautiful music, the most beautiful music I have ever heard."

"It must be. You are absolutely radiant."

"You know, Josh, I don't think I'm going to be alone."

"No, I don't think you will be."

"Oh, Josh, I want to go. Do you think it will be all right if I go? They are calling me. There is a light, and a path, and the music. Do you mind, Josh, do you mind if I leave you?"

"No, I won't mind. I will stay here with you until you go."

"Will you keep holding me?"

"If you want me to."

"Please. Josh?"

"Yes?"

"Do you know what the name Joshua means?"

"I do."

"What does it mean?"

"It means, the Lord saves."

Lord, in you the words of the prophets are fulfilled, the time is complete, and the kingdom of God is near. Open me to those whom others refuse to touch: the poor and homeless, the lonely and forgotten, those who are living in a strange land among people they do not know, those who are imprisoned by fear, prejudice or jealousy, those whose bodies harbor the effects of sickness and pain. Broaden my vision so that I see not only the disease but also the dis-ease of society. Place in my hands the scroll of commitment, fill my heart with your amazing compassion, and fill my spirit with faithful zeal. Amen.

Reruns

Theme: compassion; sensitivity
Scripture: Exodus 3:7-10; Jude 1:20-26
Season: Lent (ABC cycles)

Stanley was a simple man, a man who lived an uncomplicated life—uncomplicated, that is, except for Miriam, his wife.

He worked hard at his eight-to-four job at the mill. When he was finished with work, he looked forward to a couple of beers with the guys, a good hot meal with the wife, and then his one pleasure: "Charlie's Angel's" reruns.

This last thing he had to fight hard for. Usually right after supper Miriam had all kinds of work lined up for Stanley to do: mow the lawn, paint the porch, clean out the garage, fix the banister, dig the garden, repair the leaking faucet...on and on the list went, seemingly without end. All Stanley wanted to do was kick off his shoes, pop the top of a brew, and watch as three beautiful women brought justice to society.

"Stanley," Miriam's voice rasped like a hacksaw blade trying to cut through quarter-inch plate steel. "Stanley, are you down there? When are you going to take the storm windows down? I swear, it will be the middle of August and we won't have a single screen up. Stanley, are you listening to me?"

"Aw Miriam, can't I have just a little quiet? Let me watch the Angels. I'll work on the windows when it's over."

"That's what you say every night. And what do you do? You fall asleep in your chair and nothing gets done."

"It'll get done, Miriam. I promise. Just let me watch my program."

Miriam's displeasure could be measured by the volume of the noise she made as she banged the pots and pans around while washing the dishes. She also muttered to herself, just loud enough to be heard but not understood.

He tuned in "Charlie's Angel's" and tuned out Miriam. "Ah, it doesn't get much better than this."

But little did Stanley or Miriam know that this evening was not going to be like any of the others.

Stanley took a drink from his can of beer, looking down the length of the can in almost the same way as one would sight a gun, and listened as Charlie spoke with the Angels and Boswell, outlining their assignment. Suddenly the picture disappeared and the screen went dark.

"Miriam, is the power off?"

"Of course not! What are you talking about?"

"The set isn't working. Right in the middle of the program everything went blank."

Stanley knew what was coming even before Miriam said it. "Aw, that's a shame. Does that mean you will be able to do the windows now?"

"Miriam, will you please get off my back? I work hard at the mill. Is it too much to ask to come home to some peace and quiet? Honestly, it just isn't fair that—"

Stanley never finished his sentence for just then the television came to life again, only the program wasn't the same.

"What is this?" Stanley asked as he reached for the remote control and started to switch channels. "That's strange, all the channels are the same."

It was strange. All the regular programming on every station had stopped. Now every channel showed another program that closely resembled a news broadcast but wasn't quite the same. "Miriam, come down here and look at this."

Miriam sensed the effect on Stanley by the tone of his voice.

She descended the stairs to their "family" room, drying her hands on a hand-towel as she walked. "What's wrong?"

Stanley didn't look up. He could not divert his eyes from the changing images on the screen.

"What are you watching? What is it? Stanley, say something."

And then both of them sat silent—not another word was spoken. Stanley and Miriam just sat and watched.

The segments were brief, but there was no missing the message. Scene followed scene...scenes of Christians fighting Moslems in Beirut, Jews fighting Arabs in Palestine, Protestants fighting Catholics in Ireland, Contras fighting Sandanistas, emaciated Ethiopians, freezing homeless, abused children, glazed-eyed drug addicts, greedy pushers, soliciting prostitutes and willing "Johns," porno shops and crack houses, forgotten elderly, exiled AIDS victims, the poor, the exiled, criminals on death row...scene after scene of human injustice, depravation, greed, and moral poverty. Stanley wiped a tear from his cheek with the back of his hand, and Miriam sniffed as she searched the pocket of her apron for her handkerchief.

Then the images changed to children laughing and playing, lovers walking hand in hand, nursing homes with parking lots filled with the cars of visitors, neighbors giving neighbors a hand, the birth of a child, successful bypass surgery.

Then, once again, the screen darkened. A voice, commanding but gentle, spoke. "You have just seen a small portion of what I see day after day. My vision has been granted to you so that you will know the truth, and the truth will set you free. This is my commandment: I am the Lord your God, you shall have no other gods. This is my commandment: Be fruitful, multiply, subdue the earth, and fill it. This is my commandment: You shall love your neighbor as yourself. This is my commandment: Love one another as I have loved you."

Stanley and Miriam sighed deeply as though taking their first life-breath. They looked at one another in wonder. A change had come over them, but it was difficult to know what it was. They just sat and stared at the blank screen. Did they really see what they thought they had seen? Was it real? Was it a dream? Was it a hoax?

"Please stay tuned," the voice came from the speaker in the set. "We are experiencing technical difficulties and have temporarily lost control of our programming. We will resume our regular schedule as soon as—"

Once again the screen sprang to life. Boswell and the Angels looked knowingly at one another as they did every night when they had completed a successful mission. "Well Charlie," Boswell said into the conference phone speaker on his desk, "that wraps it up."

Stanley pressed the power button on his remote control. A faint click signaled that the power had been turned off. He picked up his half-filled can of warm beer.

Miriam looked up. ""Stanley, where are you going?"

"It's time to put the screens in the window. The fresh air will feel good."

AUTHOR'S NOTE: This story grew out of an image that was suggested by Father Ed Hays in the volume 8 number 2 issue of *The Forest Letter.* In it he wrote:

> Television is God's vision. Technology has given us that Godly vision which enables us to see around the world, to see oppression, greed and vicious killing in almost every area of this small planet. As a result of this marvel of the 20th century, we now see a tiny fraction of what our Divine Parent sees.

With thanks to Ed Hays!

Lord, it seems like life is a series of reruns: we've seen the events, we know the plots, and we're just filling time. But in you all is fresh and alive, filled with truth, grace, and joy. You have given us the commandments to live in love, to hate what is evil and cling to what is good. Give me a glimpse of that vision of your kingdom where the lion shall lie down with the lamb, and the child can play over the adder's nest. Be my ray of light and fill me with your joy. Call me to faithfulness and strengthen me with your Holy Zeal. Amen.

Trouble in Paradise

Theme: compassion; God's passion
Scripture: Genesis 3:9-15
Season: Pentecost (B cycle)

There was trouble in paradise. Oh, it wasn't so obvious that the casual observer would know that something was wrong. It was just that, well, strange things were taking place. For one thing everything was quiet. Usually one would hear (if one could have been present) the excited chatter of Eve and Adam as they made their discoveries. Eden was brim full of surprises, not the least of which were all the nuances of their newly formed relationship. Like newborn babes they delighted in the unveiling of all that life had in store for them. Their exhilarated chatter was a constant accompaniment to the sounds made by the birds, animals, and insects of this new world.

But not now. The birds, animals, and insects were doing their part. But all else was quiet—too quiet. Something was wrong.

Another clue that things were amiss was that the Lord was looking for Adam. That never happened before. Almost like clockwork, Adam or Eve would be there to greet God almost as soon as the Lord's presence in the garden was determined. But now Yahweh was searching, calling,

"Adam, Eve, where are you?" The presence of God could be felt traversing paths, pushing through the undergrowth, looking everywhere conceivable. But Adam and Eve could not be found; neither would they answer the Lord's call.

A keen observer would quickly discover why they could not be found. The simple explanation was that they were hiding—yes, hiding—deliberately, for fear that God would see them. Imagine that! There certainly was trouble in paradise.

From behind the trees and bushes, the searching eyes of the first parents peered to see where Yahweh was looking. When Jehovah came too close, the shadows of two figures would hustle to new hiding places far from the pursuing presence of God.

On into the evening this game of hide-and-seek continued. The great Lord Almighty called for the children created in God's own image, and they diligently found new places to hide. It was obvious that Adam and Eve did not want to talk with Jehovah. There certainly was trouble in paradise.

Finally, "Ah, there you are, my children," shouted the Lord when he spotted the top of Adam's head above a bush; Eve stepped out from her hiding place but remained well in the shadows of the forest. "Come out, come out. It's time for our little stroll and chat. We have so much to talk about, and I have much to learn from you. Please, let us begin."

Adam stood and made sure that the bush was high enough to provide the shield of modesty he sought. "Uh, if it's all the same to you, Lord, I think I would like to stay right here."

"Yeh, me too," came the voice from the shadows.

"What is the matter? You both are acting rather oddly."This time Eve spoke: "Oh, it really isn't anything to be alarmed about. It's just that Adam and I would feel, oh, you know, shall we say more comfortable where we are. Why don't you just stay there and we'll talk."

"I do not understand what is taking place. Why are you hiding behind that scrubby little bush, Adam? And Eve, you're so deep into the shadows that I can hardly see you. Come out here where we can be together."

Adam coughed nervously. "Well, Lord, you see, it's just that we're, uh, that is to say that Eve and I happen to be, (cough), what I am trying to say..."

"Adam! Spit it out. For goodness sake, tell me what you're trying to say."

"We're naked," Adam blurted.

The fire of a thousand volcanoes flashed in the eyes of Yahweh. "Who told you you were naked?" the Lord's voice crashed with the force of thunder. The very earth upon which they stood trembled. Adam and Eve quickly ducked back into their hiding places.

Then all was quiet. Not even the birds or the animals nor the insects sang their songs. Everything was just still—deathly still. The only sound that was heard above the powerful silence was that of someone weeping softly.

With fearful anticipation, Adam peeked out from between the branches of the bush and what he saw filled him with absolute terror. Now there really was trouble in paradise. What he saw was the Mighty Lord sitting on a rock, bent forward, face in hands, weeping.

Hesitantly both Adam and Eve stepped out of their hiding places and tiptoed toward the Lord. Hearing them approach, Jehovah straightened slowly and said, almost in a whisper, "Adam. Eve. You ate the forbidden fruit, didn't you?" Rocking back and forth the Lord continued, "Oh, oh, why? Why did you do it? Why?"

"Well, don't blame me," Adam said. "I was content to leave well enough alone. But this woman you gave me—she's the one at fault. She gave me the fruit to eat, and you know how persistent women can be."

The Lord gave him a puzzled look.

"Sorry. I forgot. Just take my word for it. Women can be very insistent. Everything has not been peaches and cream for me here, you know. 'Adam do this.' 'Adam do that.' That's how it all happened. She came sashaying in here with this fruit in her hand. 'Here, taste this,' she said, 'it's good.' What choice did I have?"

"Now wait just a minute," said Eve crossly, "I am not going to take all the blame for this. I was tricked. I was seduced..." Adam gave her a startled look... "by this serpent that you..." Eve pointed at the Lord... "put here in this garden. If you want to blame someone, blame the serpent. 'Go ahead. Eat it. It won't hurt you. Don't worry, you won't die. You'll just be more like God, that's all.' I have never before heard such a load of—"

God's hand rose for silence. With eyes filled with a hurt deeper than that which could ever be experienced, the Lord looked upon those who bore the very image of Yahweh. "Please, no more. You cannot undo what was done by blaming one another. The point is, you have chosen to abandon your innocence."

To the serpent the Lord said, "Humankind will fear you from this time on. When they see you they will attempt to crush your head with their heel and you shall strike at them. No more shall you tempt others for people will turn away from you and flee."

Adam stood, head bowed, toes tracing meaningless designs in the dirt. "And you, Adam, shall provide food and home for your family. But no longer will it be Paradise. You will till the soil and the soil will resist you. You will plant and harvest but not without toil and hardship. By the sweat of your brow you shall live."

And then to Eve: "Oh Eve, lovely Eve. The one who was created to stand with her husband. You shall do so and you shall bring forth children. It shall be your desire. But in pain shall you give birth. And you shall be in pain further still when that which you love will leave."

The Lord stood and turned to walk out of paradise. "And I shall have to find a way to undo what has been done. My suffering is deep. And it will continue until the ransom can be paid, until the salvation can be won, until redemption prevails. I shall suffer with my children. But I shall bring them back again. I will bear their burden even if I have to die for them. My suffering will not cease until that day when all will be made right again. This indeed is a terror-full day. Today there was trouble in Paradise."

God, your tears continue to flow for your children who are not content to be what you have made them. I am truly sorry for thinking and acting that to be created "a little lower than the angels" is not high enough. My sins and the sins of all people have brought pain to you. My fear of you has always been of your wrath, your anger, your ability to end what only you have begun. But, now I know a greater fear: that of hurting you. I pray for compassion, the sensitivity to be able to "suffer with" those whose lives are torn and painful. As I contemplate your tears of compassion, may I also grieve and lament with you for the tears I have caused. And, in the end, may I rejoice that your will is life and not death and that, when creation fell, you found a way to restore it through your Son in whose name I pray. Amen.

The Light in the Lantern

Theme: revelations of self; God's presence
Scripture: Deuteronomy 4:32-34,39-40, 8:2-3,14-16
Season: Trinity Sunday (A)

He was an old man. The weight of his tired, bent body was borne by the stout walking staff he held with his right hand. Though old, his eyes glistened with life from the fire that burned from within. His left hand held the handle of a lantern—a lantern not unlike those carried by travelers, yet strangely different. For one thing, the light that shone from its depth forever changed—its color, its intensity, its pulsating patterns. But the strangest phenomena was that no visible source of its light could be seen. It appeared as though it came from nowhere and everywhere.

He was an old man.

He was a holy man.

He stood in the doorway of the inn, tired from the day's journey, weary from life's pilgrimage. His eyes slowly moved from table to table, seeking out a place where he could rest his body and satisfy the hunger that gnawed at his empty stomach.

The Inn of the Broken Spoke was crowded. The voices of the patrons produced such a cacophony that the old man winced. Scullery maids carried tankards of ale, carafes of

wine, and plates of hot food to the hungry travelers, all of whom, like the holy man, paused to rest at the end of the day.

After a while he saw an empty space at a table from which the loudest noise came. He made his way between people and tables until he reached the bench with the open space. Slowly he lowered himself, bent forward to place his staff at his feet, and set the lantern on the greasy table top.

He looked at those who shared his table and as his glance stopped at each one the dancing light in the lantern changed.

A serving girl walked past, and the most boisterous member of the party, a huge, loud, crude, burly man, grabbed her around the waist and pulled her onto his lap.

"C'mere wench," he slurred lustily, "and satisfy my hunger."

She struggled to escape the hold he had on her. "Please, sir, let me go. I have much work to do. If my master sees me sitting down he will punish me."

"Blast your bloody master," he bellowed, "you are what I need right now."

As the old man watched, the lamp's light dimmed until it appeared that it was about to be snuffed out.

"Let her go, Bruno!" The voice came from a young man who sat directly across the table from the holy man. His voice carried authority but trembled slightly as though he had said a fearful thing.

Bruno glared at the young man; their eyes locked. After a few seconds, the maid was released and rushed off in the direction of the kitchen.

"What's wrong with you?" Bruno exploded. "You're not my conscience. When are you going to stop trying to rescue everyone? First it was the old woman you gave money to this morning. Then you had to stop and help a farmer fix his plow. Now this. It's getting so I can't stand to have you around anymore. Well, I don't care what you say. That wench is going to be mine."

The holy man looked at the young man, whose face was now flushed with anger and embarrassment.

The holy man spoke. "What you did today was a good thing. Do not be ashamed." He moved the lantern in front of the young man. "Here, look into my lantern's light."

The young man lifted the lantern and stared. The light ceased pulsating. A steady, brilliant, golden glow bathed his face. He smiled and gazed with wonder as the light glowed brightly.

After a while he placed the lantern on the table and the light took up its pulsating dance.

Another man, much older than his companions but not as old as the holy man, turned toward Bruno. "Don't be so hard on Richard. He's young and has much to learn."

"Shut up, you old fool," Bruno thundered, "you're not any better. If you hadn't been so honest, we wouldn't have to be in this flea-bitten garbage pile."

"I couldn't cheat those people. They were strangers and did not understand our money. It would have been wrong to take advantage of them."

"Bah, they could have afforded it. We're the ones without money."

Again the holy man moved the lantern and bid the other to look into its light, and again the light grew brighter and steady, this time a brilliant orange. The old man who looked into its light wore an expression of awe.

"Here, let me look at the bloody lamp," Bruno demanded as he snatched it from the hands of his companion.

Before he got it to his eyes, the light went out.

"I don't see anything in there. It's dark and empty. Old man, you have a cheap lantern. The slightest breeze snuffed the flame."

"Oh, the light hasn't been extinguished," replied the holy man.

"Are you blind as well as crazy? The devil take me if I can see any light inside." Bruno all but threw the lantern onto the table. It rocked in place, but when it stopped the lantern was giving forth dancing rays of changing light.

"What the—?" Bruno started, but was cut off by the holy man.

"You all have looked into the lantern's light," he said, "and what you saw was the light from within your own heart. You, Richard, your heart glows with kindness. And you," he turned to the older of the three, "your heart shines with honesty. But you, Bruno, your heart is cold and dark and black as night. You are concerned only about yourself. You are cruel, selfish, and ruthless. What you saw was the interior of your heart. But even in you, somewhere, there is some good, no matter how small it may be."

Bruno sat in stunned silence. He thought to himself, "Is it so? Is my heart that dark? What is this holy man telling me?"

He picked up the lantern once again; his hands trembled with fear. The light dimmed, and sadness creased his face as he looked into the depths of the lantern. He was about to return it to its owner when he stopped. He brought the lantern close to his eyes. There, in the deepest interior he saw it: a tiny pin point of light, a light that not even the darkness of his heart could overcome.

O Holy Light, who illumines even the darkness of the hearts of people and whose light cannot be overcome, shine within me and through me. As I am bathed in your rays, penetrate even the deepest corners of my heart, my spirit, my mind, my life, and my world. And when it seems as though the Prince of Darkness has extinguished even the Light of the World, flood me with your brilliance. Shine upon the path of my journey. Inspire me and kindle within me the spark that will burn brightly with joy and service. And when that flame is struck, keep me from wanting it for myself by covering it but give me strength to spend it for others. O Holy Light, illumine me. Amen.

The Judgment of the Village

Theme: acceptance; hospitality; judgment; ministry to Christ
Scripture: Matthew 25:31-46
Season: Pentecost (27th Sunday, A cycle)

Once upon a time, in a land far, far away, there was a small village nestled deep in a valley. It was a quiet village; a peaceful village; a village where everything happened according to schedules and plans. The seasons came and went with clockwork regularity; the rain fell and the sun shined in just the right proportions; the crops grew and were harvested right on time and babies were born in nine months to the day.

Life in this village was very predictable. That made the mayor's job all the easier. Because it always rained at the right time, all holidays were celebrated with parades and the mayor could issue his proclamations knowing that they would be carried out without fail. Yes, everything was just fine in this village. Shoelaces never broke when people were in a hurry; children respected their elders; watched pots boiled; law and order prevailed; and it never, no never, rained on parades.

Everyone knew everybody else in the village. They all went to the same school, the same church, and attended the same festivals. The young men married young women from the village and they stayed there carrying on the traditions of the parents. Yes, indeed, it was a quiet, tranquil, peaceful little village.

Then, one day, a stranger came to town. Everyone knew he was a stranger. He looked different, he acted different, he even talked different.

At first the villagers ignored him. Perhaps they thought that if they would not pay any attention to him he would go away. So, they went about their own business, doing what they did day after day, year after year.

But the stranger did not go away. Everyday in the market place, on the streets, at picnics, he was there. Of course no one spoke to him. They would pass him by without so much as a "good day," or "hello." And he would just look at them with deep sadness in his eyes and wait with hope in his heart that someone would talk to him, welcome him, offer him a piece of chicken or a slice of cheese from their picnic basket.

All of this made the villagers uneasy because they were not certain that they were doing the right thing. All they knew was that he was a stranger, and the way they lived did not take the stranger into account.

Then one day the villagers noticed some strange things happening. It all started when the village wizard ran into the mayor's office and, scarcely able to catch his breath, informed his honor that it was going to rain on Saturday.

"What?!" his honor thundered, "It can't rain on Saturday. That's the day for our Founder's Day celebration and we are going to have a parade. Besides, I have already made the proclamation!"

Almost at the same time this was going on, the vicar was getting ready for a meeting with a young couple who wanted to get married. He was already late for the meeting, and his shoelace broke.

"Oh dear, what shall I do?" he fretted. "This has never happened before. Oh what shall I do?"

What he did was hurry off to the meeting with one shoe tied and one shoe not tied; one shoe firmly held onto his foot and the other shoe flopped as he walked. Step *flop*. Step *flop*. People stepped aside to see and hear this odd sight, many having a hard time keeping from laughing.

Now, as if that was not enough, on the other side of the village, in the cottage closest to the mountain, the widow Hastings was preparing stew for her seven children as she did every day at noon. She filled the big black kettle with water and put it on the fire to boil. Then she pulled up a stool and sat and watched...and watched...and watched; and the water did not boil.

"Hmmm," she said to the dancing flames under the pot, "that's strange. Every other day when I watch the kettle the water boils, but today it will not. I better report this to the mayor."

So, the widow Hastings gathered her children together and marched off to the mayor's office on the other side of the village. On the way she met others who were going to the same place for different reasons. Farmer Brown found that his potato crop was not ready to be harvested; Joe the blacksmith hit his thumb with his hammer; Mr. Samuel's son did not put the garbage out the night before when he was supposed to. The group of people grew as it moved toward the mayor's office.

His honor was already on his balcony of pronouncements when he saw all the people coming his way. "Oh dear, oh dear," he whimpered, "they're coming to oust me from office. I know it. I can see it in their eyes. It has never happened before. Oh dear!"

But much to his relief, he soon discovered that the people had other concerns that brought them to the village square. They came because they did not understand.

They all told their stories—strange stories—and they wondered why? Why were these things happening? Did they ever happen (here or anywhere else) before? Oh, the questions they asked were so deep and profound that they gave the mayor a headache.

After a while he held up his hands for silence. A hush fell over the people. (It always does when the mayor holds up his hands). It was a signal that he was about to say something and the people wanted to hear what it was (even though it seldom was very important). "Citizens," he said in his best mayor's voice, "I have heard your questions and..." Everyone leaned forward to hear. "...I will have to think about it."

So the leader of the village withdrew to his chamber of contemplation where he thought and thought and thought until his headache grew worse. He reasoned to himself: "Odd things are happening here; they have not happened before as far as I can remember. Something is different; something must be causing...*The stranger!*"

He donned his mayor's frock encrusted with the mayor's medals, his mayor's sash of many colors, and his mayor's hat, and he marched out of his office into the open square."Follow me," he commanded the crowd.

The large army of people wound their way through the streets of the village behind their mayor, who marched like a general in front of his troops. Soon they were all in straight lines and walking in step with their mayor. They marched and they marched until they found the one who the mayor was sure was bringing these strange happenings to his village.

"You," his honor pronounced with an accusing finger pointed, "you are not one of us. You do not know our ways. You do not believe our beliefs. You do not dress with our clothing. You do not speak with our accent. You do not live in our houses, plow our fields, belong to our church. You are the cause of these happenings."

The stranger stood straight and tall. It seemed as though he towered over everyone that was there. He looked straight into the eyes of those who had gathered before him and his gaze burned deep inside of them. The mayor, for the first time in his life, felt his knees knock and he started to sweat the perspiration of fear.

"I did not cause those things to happen today. You brought them on yourselves with your lives that leave no room for the unexpected. I did nothing to you. But what you did to me shall be a judgment upon your village."

His honor, the mayor, started to sputter. "What we did to you! We didn't do anything to you."

"Precisely," the stranger said. "I was a stranger in your midst and you did not welcome me. I went to your picnics and you did not feed me. I was alone and no one visited me. I came among you as someone you do not know and you accuse me of causing strange things to happen. Your life appeared to be good and comfortable until the unexpected came and visited you. You know only what you see and what makes you comfortable. I know what is in your hearts."

And the stranger turned and started to walk away from the village. He took a few steps, stopped and stomped his feet against the hard surface of the road. The last thing the villagers saw was the dust of their village fall from his feet.

Lord, when did I see thee and care for thee, or not reach out to thee? How easily this question rolls off of my tongue but how difficult it is to admit that more often than not I have turned aside for my own comfort. The hungry are not fed because I have not provided food. The naked are not clothed because I expect the thrift stores and social agencies to do it for me. The lonely are not visited because I am too busy with a more important agenda. Those in bondage are not free because I am comfortable in my freedom. I know that I cannot do everything by myself, but that does not give me an excuse to do nothing. You have called me to see your presence in the faces of those whom you came to love and save. You have given me the example. Give me the strength to follow where you have led. Amen.

The Report

Theme: good over evil; Satan; temptation
Scripture: Matthew 4:1-11; Mark 1:12-13; Luke 4:1-13
Season: Lent (1st Sunday, ABC cycles)

> Now there was a day when the sons of God came to present themselves before the Lord, and Satan also came among them. The Lord said to Satan, "Whence have you come?" Satan answered the Lord, "From going to and fro on the earth, and from walking up and down on it" (Job 1:6-7, R.S.V.).

"And how does it go with my people on earth?"

"Well, Lord," Satan replied as he took his place at the conference table, "that all depends on how you look at things. From my perspective, everything is just fine. But, if I were you—which I am not—I would start to get a little worried."

"How so? Explain yourself."

"Okay. It's just that..."

"Go on."

"Let me put it this way. I'm not sure I really want to risk telling you. I know what your anger is like. Promise not to throw one of your tantrums?"

"No, Lucifer, you don't have to worry. Just tell me how you are finding things among the people who bear our image."

Satan cleared his throat and started giving his account. "Let's begin with how they treat each other. That has always been a big concern of yours. In fact the Commandments you gave to that fellow Moses were weighted heavily on the side of community. And much of what your Son taught focused on love for one's neighbor."

"I'm aware of all of that. From the beginning I wanted my people to live together in peace and harmony."

"Right! It didn't last long, though, did it? When given a choice between your will and my temptations, you really didn't stand a chance. That was apparent when...oh, what's her name?...Eve, that's it...when Eve decided to risk everything just to have a taste of the fruit of the knowledge of good and evil. From then on, it has been all down hill. My latest tour indicates that things are going from bad to worse."

"Tell me what you are finding."

"Are you sure you want to hear this?"

"No, not really. But tell me anyway."

"For starters there is something people are calling abuse. There seems to be so little regard for life—others' and their own—that they are dumping all kinds of abuse on themselves. It comes in many forms: mental abuse, physical abuse, emotional abuse, even spiritual abuse. There is no regard for sex or age. You really don't want to know the shape this abuse is taking. Some of it even makes me sick."

The Lord sighed. "I shouldn't be surprised. If they could dream up something like a cross they are probably capable of doing almost anything."

"That's not all. You have your regular run-of-the-mill wars and conflicts. They've been around so long now I almost take them for granted. But they also seem to be at war with themselves. They are literally destroying themselves while they try to find the meaning of life or in their search for happiness. People work so hard at recreation that they are killing themselves in the process. Major attractions are what life can offer them materially and physically. Hedonism has had a rebirth. Don't even ask about the spiritual."

The Lord's face clouded with sadness. For the longest time, they sat in silence.

Satan took out a small notebook and turned a number of pages until he found the one he was looking for. "Let's see now," he continued, "I've made a few notes here. First there is affliction. Is there ever affliction! 'Do to others before they do to you.' That seems to be the motto of the times. Cruelty, injustice, insensitivity, inhumanity, persecution, prejudice. I think you are getting the picture."

The Lord simply nodded his head.

"Next there is hunger. The amazing thing is that the problem is not so much the lack of food as it is the distribution of food. A couple of countries could probably feed the world but to do so would upset the economic system. In order to preserve that economic balance people die of starvation; children's bellies are swollen from malnutrition; diseases are wiping out groups of people. And to think...this would not have to be.

"Then there is a new problem. Well, it's not all that new; it's just that people are more aware of its existence because it affects so many. It is called homelessness: no place to live; no protection from the weather; no adequate clothing. It is a real pathetic sight. One used to almost expect it in places like Calcutta and Bombay. But now it's found in places like New York, Washington, Berlin, and London.

"We won't have to get into the myriad of ways in which life is placed in peril or the profusion of wars. No sir, it is not a pretty picture. Everything is coming loose."

Satan closed his notebook and silence filled the room. All who had gathered dared not even to breathe; no one stirred. In fact, it is a natural law that when it gets this quiet someone has to cough—and no one did.

But suddenly Satan jumped up. He started to dance and laugh. "Ha, ha, you old fox. I've finally got you. I've won! I've won! I've won! It has taken all these years and untold trials but I finally have you. You have lost. Everything has been for naught. You just can't stand up to me any more. You're washed up, finished, kaput. I have finally succeeded in taking your people away from you."

The Lord's fist came down upon the tabletop with a thundering blow. Satan stopped his dance in mid-step and nearly fell on hisface. "No!" the Lord bellowed, "you have not won. You haven't even learned anything all these eons. You think because of the foolishness of women and men that we are separated. You still don't understand, do you? They are my people not because of their faithfulness or faithlessness; not because they are good or bad; not because they deserve it or not. They are my people because of what I do for them. I forgive them. I have mercy on them. I chastise them. I lead them. But most of all, you silly imp, I love them, something of which you are incapable of knowing. Be gone, Satan. Leave this place. Go back to where you came from."

Satan slowly turned and sulked toward the door. Just as his hand reached for the door hasp he was stopped by the voice of the Lord.

"Satan."

Old Beelzebul turned.

"Remember this, O evil one, and remember it well. There is nothing, *nothing*, that will separate me from my people or my love for them. You don't stand a snowball's chance in hell of making it any different."

You won, Lord. Yet I live my life as though there is some doubt. I fail to see that you are in control even though all else seems to be falling apart. I look at the suffering in the world and wonder why you don't do something about it, forgetting that in Jesus you have. I blame you for conditions because it is too painful to realize that it is our sin that is at fault. I claim you for my own and ignore your claim on all of creation. Yet you are patient with me. Lord, I thank you that in spite of everything and through it all your love binds us together and nothing can or will be able to separate us. Amen.

Sal's Tavern

Theme: encountering the living Christ; lost and found
Scripture: Luke 15:1-32
Season: Pentecost (16th Sunday, C cycle)

Dan had been lost before. Once when he was five years old, he had become separated from his parents while they shopped for gifts in a crowded department store. He cried for all he was worth until his father scooped him up in his arms and hugged him tight. What frightened him most was to be lost in the sea of legs. He still had nightmares in which he saw only knobby kneecaps.

Then there was the time when, as a teenager, he was on a hike with his youth group. He and his girlfriend had an argument and Dan ran off by himself. It wasn't long before he realized that he didn't know where he was. He walked and walked but nothing looked familiar. Wisely, after a while, he just sat down. It wasn't long before Bill, the youth advisor, found him. As they walked back to where the others were waiting, they had a talk about how love can hurt and the dangers of acting out. Fortunately Dan had walked in a circle, and they were just a little distance from the others.

Now he was lost again. He couldn't pinpoint the date or hour when it had begun. All he knew was that it started with the first deception. Dan was frightened at first. But he possessed an uncanny knack for being able to cover up. Before long, deceiving others came naturally. First he did it only at work, then with his wife, now his children. It was almost at the point where it was getting hard for Dan to distinguish between what was fact and what was deception. These two worlds were closely woven together, and he lived mostly by wit and cunning. So far no one had found him out. But the ax was always ready to fall. When it did it would be big-time trouble for him.

So, there was only one thing to do. Dan tried to lose himself even more at Sal's Tavern.

"Hey Charlie, how about setting up another round," Dan said to the barkeeper, who was drying glasses.

"I don't know, Mr. H," Charlie said, "you've already had pretty many."

"Nonsense, I'm as good as the moment I came in." Dan didn't tell the bartender that this was the third watering hole he had visited that night. "Look, I can still touch my nose."

Dan closed his eyes, extended his right arm out to the side and slowly brought his finger toward his face. He missed, the finger landing halfway between the tip of his nose and his brow line. "Wait a minute, give a guy a chance. That one was just for practice."

He tried again. This time his finger slipped under his nose. Dan started to giggle. The night was beginning to take its toll. "Hold on, everyone gets at least three chances." He poked himself in the eye.

Dan was laughing uncontrollably. "Well, at least I was close. Come on, Charlie, pour me another. I'm not driving. Come to think about it, I'm in no shape to walk either. Here, you take this money," he placed a twenty-dollar bill down on the bar, "and call me a cab when I leave. Just give the driver my address and tell him to stand me up at my front door."

"Well, just one more, Mr. H. That's the last one. Besides, I must close up."

"Since this is the last one, then, you better make it a double. Can't go home dry, can we?"

"I'm afraid not, Mr. H. One drink is all it's going to be."

Charlie poured the amber liquid into a clean glass, reached under the bar, and brought up two bowls, one with peanuts and the other with popcorn. "Here's something to eat, too. You really should eat when you drink."

Dan had been eating. The floor around his stool was littered with peanut shells and the front of his suit was flecked with pieces of shell and peanut skins.

He reached into the bowl and took out a peanut. He squeezed the shell too hard, and the nut shot out and nearly hit Charlie in the back. Dan giggled so hard he almost fell off the stool.

"Mind if I sit here?"

Dan let out a little yelp. "Good God, man, you scared me. Where did you come from?"

"Sorry I scared you. I just wanted to know if you minded if I sat here next to you."

The stranger was shabbily dressed. His scuffed shoes stuck out beneath trouser legs that looked as though they had never been touched by an iron. An overcoat a couple sizes too large covered his thin frame. And a brimmed hat was pulled down to cover his eyes. Dan wasn't sure about this one.

Dan looked around him. The place was deserted except for Charlie, the stranger, and himself.

"Look, if you don't mind, there are lots of places for you to sit. Why don't you go somewhere else?"

"I didn't ask you if I could sit anywhere else. I asked you if you minded if I sat here, next to you."

"Well if you must. But let me alone. I don't want to talk."

"Are you sure you don't want to talk? Sometimes you feel better after you share what's bothering you with others."

"Look, Bud, I don't know who you are or what you're trying to prove but I want you to leave me alone. If I wanted to talk I would have gone to my shrink, or better yet, talked to Charlie here."

"Okay, if that's the way you want it."

There was a quiet pause that was finally broken when the stranger said, "Well, Dan, you really fouled things up good this time, didn't you?"

Dan, in the midst of taking a sip, started to choke and cough.

"How do you know my name? What's your game, anyway?"

"How I know your name isn't important. And, believe me, this is no game. I've been looking for you. In fact I'm not the only one that's been looking for you. You can thank the good Lord that I found you first. Now, there is some hope—that is, if you are willing to hear what I have to say."

"It looks as though I don't have much of a choice, do I? Mind if I drink while you talk?"

"It's up to you, friend, but you may want to put that glass down, because what I have to say to you is important. In fact, you might say it is a matter of life and death."

"Why do I have the feeling that I am in a *Twilight Zone* movie? Aren't you being a little melodramatic?"

"You may think so. But I'm serious. Dan, you are always in the process of being lost. You are surrounded by people who love you and respect you, but you deliberately separate yourself from them, like you did in the department store when you were a child. Or when someone tries to get close to you you push them off, afraid of being hurt like you were as a teen, and run away into areas that you are not familiar with. You are so bent on success that you have forgotten that one important ingredient known as faithfulness.

"You like to believe that if you were found out, your whole world would crumble. Oh, sure, it would be uncomfortable for a while. But look at those people you are running from. They are waiting for you to loosen up and let go. They want to help you, to love you, to forgive you, and to support you."

Dan moved his lips, but nothing came out. How could a stranger know so much about him? His head was spinning, not so much from his drink as from what was taking place. He felt as though his whole life was passing before him, as though this stranger knew him, could read him like a book.

Dan tried to turn away, but the stranger took both of Dan's hands in his own. His grip was firm; it even hurt a little. Something hard was pressing against the palm of his right hand. Dan felt himself being drawn closer and closer. He felt both comfort and fear.

The stranger slowly lifted his head so that the dim light from behind the bar shone on his face. Dan gasped. What he saw sent a chill up his spine. He was frozen in wonder. First he saw the face of his father just the way he looked when he found the sobbing child who had been separated from the ones he loved so much. It was filled with warmth and compassion, a look that said, "It's okay. You're not lost. We're here and we will not let you go." Then Dan saw the real face of this advisor who had just shared his pain and anger. It was the look of understanding, of wisdom, and of patience. It knew how love found and lost can hurt. It acknowledged the foolishness of impulsiveness. But it also knew that all would be healed—that life will continue and hope will win. And then he saw the face of...

"No," Dan said unbelievingly as he pulled his hands away. "You...you...you're..."

"I know who I am, Dan. And now that you know who I am, you also know who else is looking for you. He will catch up with you someday. I just want you to be prepared. It is not important who I am. What is important is that you know who you are. You are special. That's why I came to you."

Dan's composure started to return. "Charlie," Dan started to shout, "Charlie, do you see who's here?"

"Who's where?" Charlie asked.

Dan turned. Sal's Tavern was deserted. "He was here," Dan said in a whisper. "I recognized him. I don't know how, but I did. He looked just the way I pictured him when I was a kid, just like all those paintings. And yet, he was different. I saw him, Charlie. I actually looked in his eyes and I saw a love so deep and wide. Charlie, I actually looked in the eyes of—"

"Come on, Mr. H, it's closing time. You're tired and had too much to drink. Why don't you go home. You'll feel different about it in the morning."

"But, you don't understand. But then, how can you? You didn't see him, did you? Maybe it was just a dream, or the alcohol. Maybe. But it was so real."

Dan moved away from the bar. He was about to put his hand in his pocket when he became aware of the object in his right hand that had been pressed against his palm when the stranger held his hand in his own. Dan slowly opened his hand and looked at the object that had been placed there. It was a small wooden cross. He held it up to the light. Something was stamped on the cross-arm of the cross. Dan squinted against the dim light as he tried to decipher what it was. As his eyes adjusted, he saw that it was a word.

And when Dan knew what it said, he knew that the meeting with the stranger was real. It read, "Found."

Amazing grace, how sweet the sound
  That saved a wretch like me.
I once was lost but now am found;
  Was blind, but now I see.

O Lord, it is when I have nothing that I realize I have everything; when I am the last I am the first; when I am lost I am found; when I am dead I am alive. There is not a place I can hide from you for you are always there, faithfully pursuing and calling me back. Thank you for not giving up on me. Thank you for being there no matter how bad a mess of things I have made. To you and you only do I give glory, for you have followed wherever I have gone and led me back to where I belong: into your open arms of love and grace. Amen.

What the Disciples Heard

Theme: enlightenment; groans of creation; sighs of the Spirit
Scripture: Romans 5:6-15
Season: Pentecost (4th and 5th Sundays, A cycle)

Once upon a time, in a land long forgotten, high in the mountains where the wind never ceased to blow and the snow never melted, lived a Holy Man. He was known as The Enlightened One. Though he never was known to come down from his hostel into the valleys and villages below, he had a great influence upon the people who lived in the realm. His wisdom was known as far as the caravan routes reached and his spiritual insight to the four corners of the earth.

His lodging was very simple and sparse. Many wondered how he could survive the harsh weather that beat against the walls of his room. He chose to live this austere life, but his disciples lived in warm and comfortable quarters.

Every year, many young men and women came to his Hostel of Enlightenment to sit at the teacher's feet and learn the secrets of spiritual discernment. Most stayed for only a few weeks because the discipline of silence and severe asceticism was too demanding. Others stayed longer but soon decided that the sacrifice was too great. However, even though nearly all left before they discovered the secrets of spiritual discernment, none returned to their world without being profoundly influenced and affected by The Enlightened One and his discipline.

With this Holy Man in the remote Hostel of Enlightenment there lived two others, a man and a woman. They were the only two who did not leave after a period of trial. Though they had not reached the state of total deprivation that was the strength of their teacher, they had freed themselves of many of the comforts that others were not willing to surrender. The secrets of Spiritual Enlightenments were slowly being revealed to them.

Step by step, stage by stage they advanced in their journey until one day they sat in the Hostel's chapel before The Enlightened One. They sat in silence as the wind sang its mournful song and caused the flames of the candles to dance. Slowly their teacher emerged from the depth of his meditation and looked at his two disciples to whom he would pass the keys of his hostel.

"You are not far from enlightenment," he said to them as they sat with eyes downcast. "You have studied the sacred writings of the world. You have seen through eyes that see beyond seeing and understood things beyond understanding. Now you must go by yourselves and surrender to the final trial that leads to enlightenment. Go and listen. Listen to things the ears cannot hear. Listen with your heart. Listen with your soul. And when you have heard, return and tell me what it was."

For many months that led to years, The Enlightened One did not see his two disciples. Young women and men came and they went. He taught and he prayed. Faces passed before him, all of them taking with them the richness of his wisdom and the peace of his spirit.

One day while the Holy Man was in his personal prayer room, he heard the door open and the soft shuffling of feet. He sensed those who entered sitting before him and settling into a state of abandonment. His disciples had returned.

When they became aware that he was ready to hear them, they started to speak with the softest and purest voices. "We have listened with our hearts, O teacher, and we have listened with our souls. We have heard, and we have come to tell you what we heard."

He smiled and nodded his head, giving them permission to continue.

First the woman spoke. "I listened with my heart and I listened with my soul, and I heard the groans of the world. It was groaning as if in travail. I listened and I heard it groaning for peace, for that time when people will live without destruction and when they would use of the world's gifts only what they needed to live. I heard the world groaning for understanding that it was created to be used as a gift and not abused in wanton and gluttonous abandonment. I heard it groan for the stewardship of those who lived upon it. It groaned with such depth that I cried, not with my eyes, but with my heart and my soul. I wanted to reach out and embrace the world and hold it close to my breast so that it would not have to groan any more. I wanted to rock it and hold it as a mother embraces her child to soothe and feed it. And I heard the world groan for my arms and warmth. At one moment I was its mother and it my child—and I groaned for the world for I was one with it."

The Enlightened One reached out and touched the brow of his spiritual daughter, his eyes filled with the joy of hearing the discovery of his disciple. His heart was full of the wonder of all he had known and experienced.

He turned his gaze to the other disciple, the man. He spoke with a softness that even caught the teacher by surprise. "I listened," he said, "with my heart and I listened with my soul, and I heard the sighs of the Spirit. It sighed with sighs too deep for words. It longed to be received, to be understood, to be given a place to live and lead and cause growth to happen. The Spirit sighed with the prayer that others would come to know its joy and peace; it sighed with fear that evil will prevail over good. Its sighs shook the very ground I sat upon and I wanted to embrace the Spirit as a father embraces his child to cast out fear, to comfort, to protect. I heard the Spirit sigh in longing for my arms so that it and I could be one."

The Holy One knew. They had heard. They heard not with their ears but with their hearts and with their souls, and what they heard were but two of the many voices of God. And now his heart was light and filled with joy because to them had been revealed the secrets of spiritual enlightenment: to be able to hear with more than ears, to see with more than eyes, to smell with more than nose, to touch with more than hands, and to be open to the voice of God, who speaks through all he has created.

Oh, to be able to hear with more than my ears and see with more than my eyes and to have the gift of enlightenment opened for me! But, I am too impatient to listen, too much in a hurry to see. I go through my life being satisfied with surface sounds and appearances and do not risk really listening—listening for the groans of creation or the sighs of the spirit—or seeing your presence in all things around me. I long to see your image and to hear your voice. Open my ears and my eyes to your hidden wonder and beauty and fill me with the gift of your presence. Amen.

Dennis Meets St. Peter

Theme: heaven; kingdom of God
Scripture: general
Season: general

"It's not at all like I pictured it," Dennis said to himself, remembering the mental images he had of heaven: the diamond-encrusted gold and silver fence that would surround it, and the Pearly Gates.

Oh, there was a fence surrounding heaven all right, only it wasn't made of precious stones and metals. It was wooden, much like a fence at a construction site, with holes cut in for people to look in (or out). Here and there slats were missing, leaving large gaping holes in the fence.

And, of course, graffiti decorated almost every available space. Dennis took time to read a few. He found a few of the well known like "Kilroy was here," "God is dead, Nitzche. Nitzche is dead, God."

But there were also a few originals.

"Receive all hope ye who enter here."

"Heaven: an ideal retirement community."

"Trespass, please."

"Enter without risk."

"Well, enough of this," he thought to himself. "It's time to see if I am going to get in or if they have other plans for me."

The Pearly Gates were not pearly at all, but it was a gate. Like the fence it was attached to, it was made of wood. Unlike the fence, it was well kept, neatly painted, the hinges sparkling from being well oiled, and free of all graffiti, except for one sign. It read, "Ring Bell" with an arrow pointing to a doorbell button much like the one his grandmother had on her front door. A small black button stuck out of a round brass frame.

Dennis pressed the button. He didn't hear anything, though he was not sure what he was expecting to hear. He pressed the bell a second time. Again, nothing happened. Just as he was going to try for the third time he noticed a small note written in pencil on the wood beneath the brass frame of the doorbell button. He had to move close to read it, for it was printed in tiny but neat block letters. It read, "Come in. The gate's open."

The shock almost overwhelmed him. All his life he was taught that he would be met at the gates of heaven and granted entrance if found worthy. But, there was no one here to meet him, no saint bent over the book of life with a calculator adding up all the credits and debits, no fanfare, no weeping and gnashing of teeth—just a simple note. "Come in. The gate's open."

He pushed, and sure enough, the gate was unlocked. But not a soul was to be seen. The place looked absolutely deserted. "What's going on?" he wondered. "Is this some kind of joke? Is heaven really a myth? If so, where am I?"

It was then that Dennis became aware of a strange but familiar sound. The sound he heard was so out of place it was weird. It sounded like the coughing and sputtering of a motor—a gasoline engine—almost like a lawnmower engine.

"Naw, it can't be. Not here!"

But, much to his surprise, it was what it sounded like: not a lawnmower but a miniature motorcycle. Dennis remembered seeing clowns in a circus riding them around the tent.

But a miniature motorcycle in heaven was not the strangest sight. What rode it was. On this small vehicle sat a very large man, his legs splaying out in either direction so that they resembled the wings of a gull without feathers.

"Hellooooooo," the driver shouted as he rode by, going a bit too fast.

Dennis blinked. This odd man's long white beard flowed behind him in the wind like the loose ends of a scarf. He was wearing a leather pilot's helmet (vintage World War I), goggles and all. And it was obvious he was having trouble keeping the speeding, sputtering cycle under control.

"I'll be right with youuuuuu..." he shouted again as he made a second pass in the opposite direction.

With difficulty he turned to make a third pass.

"...as soon as I figure ooooout..."

A fourth pass.

"...how to stoooooop."

With that the cycle veered off course, climbed a steep embankment, stalled, tipped over, and rolled back down, with the driver still holding on for dear life.

When the dust cleared, the tall man stood up, smoothed his wrinkled robe, and started to limp toward Dennis, whose mouth hung open in disbelief. As the man approached, he lifted the goggles and removed the old leather helmet, rolled it up, and put it inside his robe. He then reached into another part of his robe and when his hand reappeared, he was holding something. This he unrolled and placed on his head. It was a bright red fez, only where the tassel was to be attached a small propeller turned lazily in the breeze.

He came up to Dennis, held out his hand, and said, "Hi! My name's Peter. Some folks call me St. Peter. Sorry I wasn't here to meet you, but I see you found my note. Since we got these little cycles we have so much fun riding around that we sometimes forget our duties."

Dennis could not take his eyes off the propeller that was slowly spinning on top of the fez.

"You're probably wondering where we got these things." All Dennis could do was nod his head.

"Well, these hats and those cycles came as a package deal. You might call it a mixed blessing. It all started out during a Founder's Day parade in Utica, New York. It was a real nice parade before the disaster."

"Disaster?" Dennis croaked, not believing this was really happening.

"Oh, yes. It was terrible. Even made the front page of *USA Today*. It seems that the throttle on the B'nai B'rith float jammed, and before they could stop the speeding mass of flowers and crepe paper it took out three marching units."

"Oh my, that's terrible."

"Yes, it was quite a mess. There they were: Tall Cedars of Lebanon, Knights of Columbus, and Shriners all over the place."

"How horrible."

"Yeh, but the good news is we got us some fancy uniforms, funny hats, and a mess of these little cycles. We were due for some new diversions. But enough of this. I guess you would like to take a look around. Want to walk or ride?"

The vision of St. Peter perched precariously on the small cycle was still fresh in Dennis' mind, so he opted for the walking tour. So, the two set off on their trek. The road followed the fence line. After a while they came upon one of the many openings in the fence. Dennis watched as someone stuck his head in from the other side. After looking around he hesitantly stepped inside.

"'Scuse me a sec," Peter said.

He walked up to the person who had just come through the gap in the fence, spoke with him, smiled, shook his hand, and pointed down the road. The newcomer started off in the opposite direction they were going.

"What was that all about?" Dennis asked when St. Peter returned.

"Oh, he decided to come in from the other side."

"What *is* on the other side?"

"Why, hell of course. I thought you knew that."

"Do you mean that..."

"...heaven and hell are separated only by a fence?"

"Yes, and that..."

"...people can come and go from either side through the holes in the fence?"

"Precisely, and how..."

"...do I know what you are going to be asking before you do? Everyone who comes in through the gate has the same look as you do and the same questions. I don't know what they are teaching you on earth, but most people aren't ready for what they find."

"But, I thought..."

"...that it would be harder to get in? Not really. You see, those who come in from the other side through the gaps in the fence want to come in. That's all that is needed. The gate's open and fence boards are missing. People stay on the other side by choice, and they come in here by choice. God's Son took care of that."

Their conversation was interrupted by the sound of music. A Dixieland band was leading a large procession. They were playing an upbeat version of "Muskrat Ramble." St. Peter started to clap in rhythm to the music. Dennis found himself keeping time by tapping his toes. When the band came abreast of St. Peter and Dennis, they came to the end of the song and without missing a beat broke into "Hold That Tiger."

To be heard, St. Peter leaned closer to Dennis. "Would you believe that every last member of that band were church organists at one time?"

"No!"

"It's true. Paid up member of the guild. They would never play anything but asthmatic pipe organs, Bach, Beethoven, Brahms, and Baroque. Now they have real swinging times."

"But, I thought..."

"...you'd be hearing harp music? *Please*. Are you serious? You want harp music—with all that plunking and twanging? You are talking about eternity here. Oh, we do have a few purists who insist on harps. We've put the harp conservatory over yonder next the boiler works. Want to go there?"

"Goodness no. I was just curious. But there is one thing that I would like to know. Where are all of the angels that are supposed to be flying around? You know, halos, wings and all that."

Almost on cue they heard: *Whump! Sprongggggg. Wheeeeee.* Dennis watched as an angel (sans wings) arched across the heavens.

Peter traced the line of flight with his finger. "See, no more wings. Traded them in quite some time back."

Thump!

"A little more to the west, Charlie," a voice shouted, "that one landed on the other side of the fence."

Peter shook his head. "We have the propulsion down pat, but the guidance system needs a lot more work. The landing is a bit rusty too."

"But how did they do it? There weren't any wings, no motor, how...?"

"Catapult," Peter answered.

Dennis smiled. "I think I am going to like it here."

Peter's face lit up with the widest grin Dennis had seen in a long time. "Great! Welcome!" he said, pumping Dennis' hand. "That's all we need to hear." He reached inside his robe and pulled out a leather pilot's helmet like the one he wore, goggles and all. "Here, put this on. I know where we can find another cycle. If you think what we saw so far is interesting, what until you see what I have in store for you next."

"What's that?" Dennis asked with excited anticipation.

"It's where we have all those preachers who thought the form of their worship was the most important thing they did."

"What are they doing now?"

"Well, friend, I don't want to ruin the surprise," Peter said with a twinkle in his eyes, "but I hope you like fun houses."

What a delight it is, Lord, to see your heavenly realm as something akin to that which your Son revealed: as a place where those who desire it will be received and where joy and celebration abound. Many times our view is austere and foreboding. We paint images of terror and wrath. Though we believe that we are saved by faith alone, we still try to construct systems of worth or accumulate credit to make us worthy. Help me to see the holy joy of eternal life where the halls of heaven still echo with your laughter when one more life walks through the gate. Amen.

Among the Pots and Pans

Theme: being yourself; gifts; ministry
Scripture: Matthew 21:33-43
Season: Pentecost (20th Sunday, A cycle)

The deep breathing of the sleeping brothers mingled with the low whisper of the cold air that leaked through the aged mortar and ill-fitted windows. The "seasoned" brothers at the Carmelite monastery had learned how to cope with the dampness and the chill. It was the new ones, the "babes" as the others referred to them, who toyed with the worth of putting up with such hardships.

Dawn had not yet broken the gathering clouds filling the near- black sky. Soon the soft sounds of sandaled feet sleepily shuffling over the immaculately scrubbed flag-stone floor and the hushed swish of the long, coarse habits would fill the labyrinthine halls as the brothers made their way to the chapel for the first of many services of the day.

But now, all was quiet and still and dark—except for one small area: the kitchen. The light from the single candle sent out a shaft that clove the darkness with the ease of a battle-axe halving an apple. A solitary figure scurried from the cooking table, where he was preparing the morning's fare (modest as it was), to the stoves and ovens that were being heated by means of burning the precious wood fuel.

Brother Lawrence worked swiftly but noiselessly. His limp, caused by an inflamed ulcer on his leg, was becoming more pronounced. He tried to compensate and hide his discomfort. His greatest fear was that the Abbe, seeing him in pain, would remove him from this holy place.

Yes, the kitchen was a holy place for Brother Lawrence. In his own mind it was his chapel, his chores the devotion, the work table the altar. As he scurried from table to pot, from oven to wooden washtub, he would be saying his prayers, reciting the psalms, and singing the plainsong chant of his liturgy.

He stopped to wipe the sweat from his brow, remembering when, after he came to the monastery situated on the rue de Vaugiard in Paris, he was given the task of scrubbing the floors. Other novitiates smiled and breathed a sigh of relief. They would have been spared this back-breaking chore. But Brother Lawrence accepted his task with the same enthusiasm as others when they were chosen to be acolytes or crucifers. Even now, when Brother Lawrence could not sleep, he would slip out of his small, sparsely furnished room and offer up his service to God on his hands and knees, scrubbing and polishing the already glistening floor.

Brother Lawrence of the Resurrection, as he had later been called, welcomed the task. There, on his knees, he prayed to the Lord Christ, walking his own Way of Sorrows.

He fit in well with those who joined him, albeit reluctantly, with these menial tasks. Most brothers, when they first arrived at the monastery, had visions of donning the elaborate vestments of the chief celebrant at the Lord's Holy Eucharist, of being the cantor who intoned the sacred psalms, of sitting in the choir blending their voices with the others in the deep, throaty tones of evensong.

But not Brother Lawrence. When approached by the Abbe to take his place at the altar during the celebration of the most Holy Sacrament, he blanched and humbly requested that he be passed by so that some other more deserving brother could take that place.

He was a puzzlement to those around him. They could not understand why he would pass up so many opportunities. They silently wondered what it was that kept him satisfied doing the things he did: the wash bucket his chalice, the coarse brush a symbol of cleansing, the offering up of supper for his fellow monks his eucharist.

Brother Lawrence never accepted a place of honor or prominence. He was content working in the kitchen, scrubbing floors, and, later in his life when his leg would no longer allow him to stand for any length of time, as the community's shoemaker.

He was a humble man, an ordinary man, who performed his tasks, no matter how menial or commonplace, as service to his Lord. Whatever he did and wherever he did it, it was performed in the presence of God. His was the simple life, and for that reason it was much more difficult than if he had taken the higher road. Among the religious he stood as a giant because he believed that his servitude freed him to become God's instrument in the hallways, the kitchen, the community garden, or the shoe repairer shop.

While others sought to be close to God at the altar, in the choir, or the library, simple, meek, humble Lawrence was close to God where he lived and toiled for others. This attitude of a servant brought him closer to the others, and he knew that when he was close to others as a servant he was close to God.

After a painful illness he died in the monastery on February 12, 1691. His life was a perfect example of a holiness that could not be contained, blazing forth from a simple creature living in obscurity and performing the most humble tasks. He profoundly influenced the lives of all who came into contact with him and, through his writings, generations of men and women after his death" (*The Practice of the Presence of God by Brother Lawrence of the Resurrection*, translated by John J. Delaney, Image Books, 1977, pages 18 and 19).

He was an ordinary man who served his Lord in an extraordinary way: just by being himself.

Lord Jesus Christ, brother, friend, companion on the journey, I have something to say that is not easy to admit. It has been such a burden and it has made my journey troublesome at times. I wonder why and often lament that I am not more than I am. I feel inferior to others. I am certainly jealous when recognition passes me by and others less deserving (by my assessment) are lifted up. I am insecure and am prone to compensate by trying to earn acceptance or recognition. And, as I am sharing this with you, I am aware that my problem is that my attention is centered in myself. Help me to know and accept the true humility of Brother Lawrence who was able to turn a kitchen table into an altar, a scrub bucket into a holy font, and the joy of serving others into the joy of serving you. You have made me what I am. May all glory and praise be yours, my Lord, and may I rejoice in being me. Amen.

The Truck Stop

Theme: coming of Christ; God's time
Scripture: Matthew 22:24-40, 25:1-13
Season: Pentecost (23rd and 24th Sundays, A cycle)

Jack was tired. It had been a long and grueling trip. And now, as he looked through the rain-splattered windshield of his Kenworth, he felt the fatigue brought on by trying to mesh together the surrealistic scene in front of him with the way he knew it was supposed to look.

"I'm getting too old for this." Jack often spoke out loud even though he was the only one in the cab of the tractor. It had become a habit used to fight off the tiredness. Lately he found himself doing it with more frequency.

"Maybe I better hang it up soon. I've been on the road—and away from home—for too many years. The kids are all grown and on their own and I missed half of their lives. Delores and I deserve some time together. I don't know how much more time I have. So, if I would be smart, I'd retire and enjoy whatever is left."

Out the side of his vision he caught sight of a familiar landmark. He sighed in relief knowing that he would soon be at the truckstop, and that meant some welcome time from behind the wheel.

"Besides," he continued his monologue, "there's just too much pressure; push, push, push. The company wants me to push my speed to make the trips in less time; I'm pushing my time behind the wheel past what is allowed; I know they pushed the weight I'm carrying. Thank goodness it's raining; if I got weighed it would mean a fine, lost time, maybe time in a local jail."

Jack's mind retraced his run that day. "I'd be home by now if I would have minded my business. Why do I always get suckered into..."

He remembered the helpless look on the face of the little old lady as she stood behind her car. The left rear tire was flat and showed signs that she had driven some distance on it after it had deflated. He knew she didn't have the strength to change it—probably didn't even know how. When he brought his rig to a stop, dismounted from the high cab, and approached her he realized her need—and her fear. She held her umbrella as one would a weapon for defense, knowing she needed help but not quite trusting this stranger: a big, burly truck driver.

Jack spoke reassuringly to her as he removed her spare from the trunk only to discover there was no auto jack. He smiled. Experience had taught him to carry one in his truck.

In a few minutes the tire was changed.

"If I might make a suggestion," Jack said, "I'd go to a garage real soon and get a new tire. This old one's shot. And, while you're at it, you better get a jack too."

He refused the ten dollars she offered, and wished her a safe journey.

The smile on his face soon faded when he remembered slamming on his brakes and fighting the wheel to control the loaded trailer pushing from behind. A small boy stood on the side of the road and watched in horror as his dog ran in front of a car and was hit. Jack cursed as he watched the driver of the car drive off without so much as slowing down. "Damn," he exclaimed as he hit the steering wheel with his fist. He bounded from his cab and grabbed the boy just as he was ready to run out into the road in the hopes of rescuing his pet.

The dog was killed instantly, and Jack just held the little boy as he sobbed his deep grief. Tears filled Jack's eyes when he remembered when his son mourned the death of a family pet. It was so hard just letting things take its course. He wanted to fix things and make it better for his son, but some things are not fixed that easily.

The boy's mother, not far away and hearing the high-pitched squeal of the tires, came to the road and found the massive arms of a stranger wrapped around her boy like a blanket. When she saw the lifeless body of their pet on the road, she knew what happened. After a while Jack looked up, saw the mother, and surrendered the boy to her. "This is going to hurt him a lot," Jack said, "be patient with him and let him cry. There's going to be a mighty big hole that is going to take some time to fill."

She nodded, smiled her appreciation, and took her son's hand as, with her other hand, she wiped a tear from her eyes.

The familiar glow of the neon sign announced that Jack was about to be able to relax. After he parked his rig, he entered the restaurant. Sal, as much a fixture as the old formica-topped counter, was serving up a hot meal to another trucker at the other end of the counter. Jack and the other trucker nodded but honored each one's need for rest and quiet. The radio was tuned, as always, to a local station that carried nothing but religious programs. A country-and-western style hymn was providing background for the quiet diner.

Jack looked around. The place was almost deserted: just Jack, the other trucker, Sal, the cook, and a young couple sitting in a corner booth, lost in love. Jack smiled. Young love always brought a smile to his lips.

"Evening, Jack," Sal greeted, "The usual?"

"No, I don't think so. What's the special tonight?"

"Meatloaf."

"How is it?"

Sal made a face.

"Give me the usual."

Just then Jack became aware that the music had stopped and someone was speaking.

"Brothers and sisters," the voice drawled, "Jesus is coming again."

A small chorus of "Amens" could be heard.

"Yes, I tell you, he's coming again. But there's something else you need to know."

The congregation became more enthusiastic.

"He's not only going to come sometime in the future. No, I say, not only some time in the future, he's coming now." This was greeted with applause. "He's coming now, and you won't even know where, when, or how. *No!* you may not even know who he is. But he's coming. He may even have been that stranger you met today."

"What do you think about that?" Sal was speaking to Jack. Jack felt as though he had just been jerked back from somewhere else. As the preacher spoke he saw the faces of a frightened little old woman, a grief-stricken child, and a grateful mother.

"What's that, Sal?"

"What do you think about what that preacher just said? Do you think the Lord is really going to come again? How can it be that Jesus just might be a stranger we happen to meet? I go to church and everything, and I've heard all of that before, but I don't know what I believe. What do you think?"

"I don't know, Sal," he said, "I haven't given it much thought."

Jack thought to himself, "Can it be? Wasn't all of that just coincidence?" Jack's brow furrowed deeply as he remembered the events of that day.

"I don't know, Sal," he repeated, "But maybe, maybe he might have something there. He just might have something."

Oh holy and hidden One, you promise to be with us always, and I believe you will come again. I pray for that sacred longing that will seek you out in those whom I meet, for that moment when you shall return and all things will be brought back into order once again. Give me the compassion that will keep me from turning my back on those whose needs I encounter. As you comforted the sorrowing, may I too be a consolation to those who weep the silent tears of grief. As you promised to come again, help me to live my life with anticipation and complete trust in your promise. Amen. Come, Lord Jesus!

Grandma Richardson's Treasure

Theme: spiritual treasure
Scripture: Luke 12:32-40
Season: Pentecost (12th Sunday, C cycle)

She was nobody's grandmother. Yet, everyone in the village called her Grandma Richardson. So, in reality she was everybody's grandmother.

Her home, like everyone else's in the village, was a modest row home. She had moved into it when she married. There she and her miner husband struggled against the odds of company-town living. Life during those days was difficult. Wages were low and the cost of living was high. Many families never escaped the debt they owed to the coal barons. There was never enough to pay both the rent and buy food at the company store.

Somehow, the Richardson family escaped the economic trap of their society. When the two boys were old enough, they went to work with their father in the deep-shaft mines from which spewed the harvested anthracite coal from deep below the surface of the earth. The youngest child, a daughter, was the only one to finish school, and she became a secretary at a local moving and storage company. The older daughter withdrew from school, like her brothers, before the seventh grade. She stayed home and helped with the chores around the house.

Grandma Richardson did not receive her honorary title until later in her life.

It all began one evening when a small knot of men, all wearing the black dirt as the emblem of their sacrifice, appeared at her front door. They all had removed their hats and most were twisting them nervously as the spokesman stepped forward and cleared his throat. She knew what had happened before the speech was made. It happened often to those who lived in that area. "Ma'am," the miner said, "we are sorry to inform you that there was an accident at number six mine. Your husband was one of those who lost his life in the accident. Please accept our deepest sympathy. If there is anything that we can do, please let our wives know."

Then, one by one, each man, carefully avoiding eye contact with the new widow, turned and wearily made his way to his own home where a hot meal of soup and bread spread with lard waited.

She was strong through it all. The viewing and the simple service conducted by the local Methodist minister was held in the parlor of the Richardson home. Following the service the closed casket was passed through the front windows (all front windows in the company homes were made large enough for caskets to easily be moved in and out) and carried to the small cemetery next to the small church.

Life went on in the Richardson household. Any mourning or shedding of tears happened behind closed doors and in absolute private. "He is in God's hands," they would say to those who offered their condolences.

Years passed slowly and with great difficulty. She still helped with the church suppers that raised the funds to support their little church. Only sickness would keep the mother and her four growing children from Sunday services. She was admired by everyone in the village for her courage and unwavering faith.

Then, on a hot August evening, there was a knock at the front door. Her heart beat rapidly. She knew. "Oh God, which one is it?" she said to her daughters, who were setting the table.

When she opened the door, she saw her youngest son standing next to the draped stretcher. The ritual of three years earlier was repeated and again the community marveled at her strength and faith. It was after that the people started to call her "Grandma," the title of supreme honor and dignity reserved only for those who have earned it.

Grandma Richardson grew older and weaker. In the spring and summer, when the weather was warm, she would sit on her front porch, rocking in her rocking chair, softly singing hymns of faith that she had learned by heart. The children in the village would often gather on her porch and she would tell them stories of the heroes and heroines of the Bible.

And then it happened again. Folks in those parts always said that bad things happened in threes. The remaining man in the household left for work that morning. But he was brought home as was his elder brother and his father before him. The mine claimed another sacrificial lamb.

Everything took place as it had before: the viewing; people filing into the parlor; gifts of cakes, pies, sandwiches; the service; and the opening of the front windows so that one more loved one could pass through on his way to the final place of rest.

The funeral was in the morning. That afternoon Grandma Richardson was in her rocking chair, softly singing her hymns of faith. At first the children stood at a distance, not knowing if it would be proper for them to visit their friend. But uncertainty gave way to courage and soon a dozen or so young folk sat cross-legged in front of Grandma Richardson, listening to the words of hymns. "Nearer my God to thee, nearer to thee," "Amazing grace, how sweet the sound," "God Himself is present, let us now adore Him." Grandma Richardson also told stories about Jesus, who is God's ultimate sign of love: "Through him we will never die, but have everlasting life."

One small child looked at the woman whose eyes danced with excitement as she talked about God's love. "Grandma Richardson," he said, "aren't you sad today?"

She bent forward, elbows on her knees and looked at every child sitting there. "Yes, dear, I am sad, very sad. It is hard to say goodbye to someone you love, and I have had to do it three times. But I have something more than sadness inside of me. I have a treasure that is worth more than all of the gold in the world."

Another child spoke up. "Oh, come on, Grandma Richardson, you are poor like the rest of us. You're kidding us, aren't you."

"No, I'm not. In part you are right, though. I can't buy anything with my treasure. But that kind of wealth isn't important. It can be lost or stolen and when it is gone I would have nothing, like everybody else. But no one can take my treasure. I can't lose it. The one thing I can do, though, is give it away. When I do, the amazing thing is, I don't have less. I have more."

"Can you give us some," a few of the children said together.

"Can I give you some? Why children, I have been giving it to you for years now. It is knowing that God loves you and that he has made one promise that is a gift, the most valuable gift in the world. He promised that no matter what happens, no matter how good or bad things may be, regardless of your joy or sorrow, he will not leave you alone or without comfort. He said, 'Lo, I will be with you always.' Yes, I am sad. But I know in my heart that this is all we need."

Well, it wasn't long after that that Grandma Richardson joined her husband and sons. A small group of children stood with their parents paying their last respects to the maiden sisters. They could not help but remember Grandma Richardson's witness and example. For truly, where your treasure is, there will your heart be also.

I thank you, Father, for those witnesses who, through their own lives and experiences, have brought me to faith and love for you. So often I believe that what I have has been acquired for myself by myself. But as I look back over my life, there is that "cloud of witnesses" who helped to shape and mold me to be what I am today. I give you special thanks for all of the "Grandma Richardsons" who remained faithful and steadfast and spoke of faith and that blessed assurance even as their own hearts were heavy. Bring to my remembrance those people who have called out of me that hidden child, and bless them with your own abundant grace, especially those I name before you. Hear my prayer, O Lord. Amen.

The Picnic

Theme: nature of Church; inclusivity
Scripture: Luke 7:1-10
Season: Pentecost (2nd Sunday, C cycle)

Jim's childhood is a painful memory. He was different from the other kids in school and in the neighborhood. Oh, just to look at him you would not see the difference. On the surface he was like any other boy. No, it wasn't until Jim would try to run or climb stairs that the difference would be seen. He could not do either very well.

His parents had Jim to the doctor a number of times, trying to find out why it was that their child could not run like other children, why climbing stairs was so laborious for him. But, the doctor was stumped too. Once he prescribed tartar and sulfur as a tonic. "That ought to straighten him out," the doctor observed. It didn't. Another time the doctor told Jim's parents that the boy was "muscle-bound" and he would grow out of it.

Well, Jim didn't grow out of it. He remained different. He couldn't run, and climbing stairs was a chore. Now, to most people this is no big deal. "So what if he can't run or climb stairs? There are other things in life than running and climbing stairs."

Not to a young boy whose friends are playing baseball, and basketball, and football. All these sports make running necessary. And not to a young boy who had to attend physical education classes in school where they played baseball, and basketball, and football. The worst part always was when they picked teams. Jim was never the captain of the team, so he never had the opportunity to pick. He was always in the group of boys who stood to the side waiting to be pointed at and then walk to the team that was being assembled.

Jim could always predict what was going to happen. He would be the last one picked. And he knew his team would say, "Aw, do we have to have him on our team again?" Physical Education class was pure torture for Jim. So, to survive the humiliation, he became skilled at faking illness and being excused from class. This was not only good for Jim; it was also a relief for the teachers and the rest of the class. That way they did not have to contend with the dilemma of a perfectly healthy boy who could not run or climb stairs.

So, Jim spent his childhood sitting on his front porch, reading books, skipping physical education class, and trying not to be hurt. The time came, however, when Jim became an adolescent and sought out those friends who would accept him as he was. It was no easy chore, for different people are not always welcomed in "normal" circles. He did find acceptance, though, in his church's youth group. They did things that Jim could do, and when he couldn't, there was always someone who saw that he was not off by himself. For the first time in his life, Jim didn't feel like a wall-flower.

Then, there came that fateful day when the youth went on a picnic. It was a glorious day. Hot dogs were roasted over an open fire. They drank birch beer on tap. The kids played, and joked, and sang songs. Then someone said, "Let's play tag!"

Jim's heart sank. "Oh God, not here too."

The group ran off down the lane to the open field where the game was to be held, leaving Jim by the side of the road where he watched with tears in his eyes. Once again his difference became a barrier. But, just as Jim was turning to go back into the grove to sit at the picnic table, his friend Melvin and a handful of others stopped and turned.

"Hey, Jim," Melvin called out. "Come on with us. You can play too. We'll wait for you."

That was the day that Jim learned that the church, the body of Christ, is that group that is willing to include everyone, even and especially those that are different; that group that is willing to wait for those who have difficulty keeping up; that group that will even adapt the game so that others can play when playing can be next to impossible.

AUTHOR'S NOTE: This is a true story. It is my story. Though it is a painful reminder of a part of my life that was difficult, I share it as a witness to both the pain of exclusivism and the joy of the spirit of inclusivism. I can know only in part what it means to be "outside," and I pray that I too will learn how important it is to have open arms, to love, and to accept all people.

Some memories are painful, Lord. I have tried to erase them from my memory, but have failed. But, I give you thanks that so much Good News has come out of the Bad News. I thank you that out of the experience of rejection by some I have had the meaning of the true church revealed to me. I thank you that out of self-doubt, others have helped me to recognize true worth. I thank you that I have been taught and believe that to be different is not a sin and that we all possess our own unique gifts. Lord, in your wisdom you did not make us all scholars or all athletes, all leaders or all laborers. I have been gifted by you as has every person who has drawn the first breath of life. O Lord, I praise you. Amen.

You Want It Made out of What?

Theme: making of gods; worshiping the giver, not the gift
Scripture: Numbers 21:4-9
Season: Lent (4th Sunday, B cycle)

The hand slowly drew back the flap on the tent just far enough to allow the bent figure to enter into the shadows. With utmost care the crouched figure tiptoed toward the sleeping figure that was curled up on the rug spread over the sand for sleeping. Deep snores and heavy breathing signaled to the intruder that his presence had not been detected. A quick glance assured him that the slumbering man's weapons were far beyond reach.

Upon reaching the prone sleeper, the dark figure noiselessly knelt and reached a trembling hand toward the unsuspecting neck of the sleeper. With one swift move he grabbed the place where the shoulders and the throat meet, squeezed and shouted, "Hey, Moz! Wake up!"

Moses bolted upright. "Huh? What...? Who...? What in tarnation is going on? Aaron, what are you doing sneaking up on me like that?"

"Well, Moz," Aaron said apologetically, "I didn't want to startle you."

"Didn't want to startle me? You nearly gave me a heart attack! Really, Aaron, sometimes I wonder whether you have both of your oars in the water. And, how many times have I told you not to call me 'Moz?' My name is Moses. Say it after me: M-O-S-E-S."

Aaron obediently and slowly repeated his brother's name. "M-O-S-E-S."

"Now," Moses continued, "to what do I attribute this unwelcome surprise? I am so tired and was having such a good sleep. I am all but worn out from running up and down the mountains here in Sinai to talk to Yahweh. You would think that He could pick a more convenient location for our meetings. But, no, that would be asking too much. Ol' Moses doesn't mind playing mountain goat. I just got back a few hours ago and I need some rest, so, come on. Out with it. It's got to be bad news because that seems to be the only thing you bring me any more. What have the Israelites done now, or what are they complaining about?"

Aaron shifted his weight. "Well, Moz, it's not exactly what the people did. And it is not exactly what they are complaining about either. It's just that, well, a sticky situation has come up that we think needs your attention."

"Well, speak up man. What is it?"

Trying to avoid looking directly at his brother, Aaron said in a near whisper, "Maybe you better see for yourself."

"Aaron, please stop playing games with me. I really am not in any mood to go through all of this. Tell me, or let me alone."

"Really, Moz, I think you ought to see this for yourself."

"Oh all right. Try and get some peace and quiet around here. Why did I have to see that burning bush? Life was so simple until the Lord got that bright idea that you and I should become the leaders of these people. I really think he had his wires crossed."

Moses continued to grumble his complaints as he slowly stood, trying to ease his sore muscles into activity. He took a few steps toward the flap, but his movement was stopped by Aaron.

"Uh, Moz, I think I better warn you that you aren't going to like what you see out there."

"Aaron, every time you come into my tent I never like what I see out there."

"Yeh, but this is kind of, well, different. You really aren't going to like it."

"Oh, come on. It can't be all that bad. Besides, I've seen pretty much in my days. Now let's see what has your tail feathers all a-flutter."

Moses pushed back the flap and was about to step outside the tent when he stopped, looked again, dropped the flap, and screamed.

"Y-e-e-i-p-e-s," he cried at the top of his voice as all of the color drained from his face. "The place is crawling with snakes."

"I tried to warn you," Aaron said weakly. "I told you you weren't going to like it."

"I hate snakes. Oh, God, why does it always have to be snakes? And, what am I going to do about it? If I step outside my tent I'll be up to my kneecaps in snakes." Then it dawned on Moses that if there were snakes on the outside of his tent, there was little to keep them from being on the inside as well. He picked up a huge club and started gingerly to take a quick survey of the room. "Oh God, I hate snakes," he repeated.

"You better do something," Aaron offered. "Some of the people have been bitten and a few have died."

"Do something? Just what did you have in mind? There's not a pest control business within miles of this wilderness."

"The elders and I had a meeting," Aaron continued, "and we think you better talk this one over with the Lord. We have concluded that we brought this on ourselves by all of our belly-aching. The people are real sorry and would be most appreciative if the Lord would take these snakes away. I think they have learned their lesson. We also think that you ought not waste too much more time."

Moses incredulously shook his head. "You want me to go and talk with Yahweh? Did it ever occur to you and your intrepid leaders that in order for me to have an audience with God I am going to have to wade though a field of writhing snakes?"

"Oh, yes. We've already thought of that and we have devised a way for you to do it with reasonable safety," Aaron responded proudly.

"Really, now? You all thought it out all by yourselves, did you? Just what do you propose is going to get me through all those snakes?"

Aaron reached into the bag he had tied around his waist. "Here, wear these."

Moses looked unbelievingly at the pair of high leather boots Aaron offered him.

"They should keep you safe as long as one of the snakes doesn't strike higher than the top of the boots. And you better walk with your hands above your head just in case one of them should be seen as a target."

Well, Moses didn't want to leave the safety of his tent, but he knew that the only way the situation would have any chance to be remedied would be through a confrontation with Yahweh. Reluctantly he prepared himself for the journey, then stepped into the leather boots that proved to be a size or two too small. His feet hurt from being cramped in them when he stood. "What I must go through to keep things on an even keel. No one would ever believe it."

He stepped outside his tent, fighting off an urge to faint at the sight of the slithering carpet that lay before him on the desert sand. "I wonder which mountain it's going to be this time," he said to himself as he looked from mountain peak to mountain peak until he found the telltale smoke and lightning.

"Oh, sure. It has to be the highest and steepest. Why can't he be satisfied with a medium-sized hill or a high sand dune?" But realizing that nothing was going to come of his complaining, he set off in the direction of the meeting place.

After what seemed to be an interminably long time, Moses finally reached his destination, weary, sore, full of bone-aching fatigue, breathless, and, all in all, not in a very good mood.

"Hi Moz! What's up?" came a voice from the dense smoke that covered the mountain peak.

"Let's not play any games," Moses countered. "I think you know darned well what's up."

"I take it the people are not too thrilled with my latest gift."

"No, they're not, and I'm not very amused by it either. You know I don't like snakes. Why does it always have to be snakes? Can't you come up with something other than snakes?"

"I really don't think so."

"Well, why not, for goodness, sake? You created so many things; what's wrong with them?"

"Well, I guess I could have used spiders, or scorpions, or lizards, or some other creepy, crawly critter."

"Right! Why didn't you?"

"Because those things give me the willies."

"Oh great. I get snakes because you're afraid of the other things."

The ground started to tremble. "Moses, are you trying to tell me how I should be handling this situation?"

Moses said quickly, "Heavens, no! Far be it from me to even suggest any such thing. It's just that it would be nice to show a little compassion and take the pressure off me."

"I hear what you're saying, Moz. But that's not why you're here. What brings you up here to the top of the mountain again?"

Sensing an opening but needing to care for a more important detail first, Moses answered, "Someday we're going to have to talk about this mountaintop fetish. Maybe you'd consider a nice tent not too far from where we camp. But, that will have to be another time. Right now I just want to let you know that you got through to my people. They realize that they were wrong complaining against you and me and they are asking for your pardon."

"So, they've come to their senses, have they? Well, that's good. And it is about time, too. You know, my patience is starting to wear a little thin. Makes me wonder if I should have left them in Egypt."

Moses coughed nervously, "If it is all the same to you, we would be deeply grateful if you would, you know, get rid of the snakes."

"Sorry. No can do."

"What?" Moses stormed, not believing what he was hearing. "What do you mean you can't take them away?"

"Just what I said. They've going to have to crawl away in their own good time and when the spirit moves them."

"Great, just great. Now what are we going to do? Do you realize what a fine mess you've gotten us into? I can see it now. I walk into the camp and announce, 'We're just going to have to put up with this little inconvenience until the snakes make up their mind to move on.' I wouldn't be surprised if the people don't take me and—"

"Moz!"

"What?"

"Chill out! I think I've got an idea that will get you over the hump."

"It's about time. What is it?"

"I want you to go back and make a likeness of a snake out of bronze and put it on a high pole. If any of the people get bitten, all they will have to do is look at the bronze serpent and they won't die."

Moses was silent for a long, long time. Finally he said, "I've got a better idea. Why don't I find a twisted stick that looks like a snake and put that on the top of the pole?"

"Gee, Moz, I don't think so."

"Well, then, how about you let me kill one of the snakes. I'll have our resident taxidermist stuff it and we'll put that on the pole."

"Sorry, it's got to be bronze."

"Bronze! Do you know what we have to go through to make a blinking bronze statue? First we have to build a furnace to melt the copper and tin *after* we've found enough copper and tin. You know, we really don't have an overabundance of those materials. When we left Egypt all we brought with us was what we could carry. Believe me, copper and tin were not high on our list of priorities. And if, just if, we can get enough copper and tin, and if we can build a furnace, then we must fashion a mold. Do you have any idea the amount of work that's going to be involved? What's our alternative?"

"Well, that depends on how much you like sharing your space with snakes."

"Oh, all right. We'll give it a try. There's no use arguing with you anyway. At least we will be able to get past this danger. I sure hope those people down in camp appreciate the trouble they've caused by not trusting you or by doubting my leadership. It really does not take too much to keep our relationship going. Maybe someday they will learn what a blessing it is to be who they are because of what you are doing. Well, I'd better start getting back. There's a lot of work ahead of us and I don't want any more of my people dying because of their foolishness. So long, Lord. Take care!"

"Bye, Moses. Be careful. You're a great leader and a good friend."

"Be seeing you."

"Yep. I'm sure we'll have to be talking some more. Oh, Moses?"

"Yes?"

"One more thing. Make sure those people realize that they are going to live because of my love and my promise. I sure would hate to have them end up worshiping that dumb bronze snake."

> In the third year of Hoshea, son of Elah, king of Israel, Hezekiah, son of Ahaz, king of Judah began to reign...He did what was right in the eyes of the Lord, just as his father David had done. He removed the high places, smashed the sacred stones and cut down the Asherah poles. He broke into pieces the bronze snake Moses had made, for up to that time the Israelites had been burning incense to it. (It was called Nehushtan.) (2 Kings 18:1,3-4, NIV). (Nehushtan sounds like the Hebrew for bronze and snake and unclean thing.)

Lord God, eternal Parent, your love and compassion are both Mother and Father to all of creation. Hear my prayer of confession for all of the times I have willingly and joyfully received your gifts and turned them into gods. I have too often knelt at the altar of the signs of your gracious fidelity while leaving my worship of you unattended. Forgive me for ignoring you, the Giver, while giving my full

attention and devotion to the "things" of your Kingdom. Open my eyes and ears to be able to understand that "You must save, and you alone." Help me to recognize that the gifts point to you and that you are the one to whom I am to give homage. And, as I am bitten by the serpents of sin, greed, idolatry, intolerance, and so many more errors, lift my eyes to the One who has been raised up before me, Jesus Christ, your Son, my Lord and that looking upon him I may see the promise of salvation. Amen.

The Solo

Theme: Christian love; faith; sin confronted, repented, forgiven
Scripture: 2 Samuel 11:26-12:10; Luke 7:36-50
Season: Pentecost (4th Sunday, C cycle)

"Really, how could she? She of all people?" Ilse Hastings did not make any attempts to hide her anger, and she found a sympathetic listener with her friend and bridge partner Alexis.

Both were scandalized by what happened during the worship service that morning.

"Alexis, we have to speak with Pastor McNeal about this. He has just gone too far. I never was too happy about singing hymns while we received the sacrament. But to let her sing that solo is just more than I can take."

"I agree, Ilse. I just don't know what our church is coming to. All of these changes we are making can't be good for society. There was a time when the church was firm and people knew where they stood. But, not anymore. After today we probably will have just anybody come in with us. And you know what kind of riff-raff is out there."

Ben Hastings and Robert stood a few paces behind their wives as they waited for the line of parishioners to file past the pastor following the service. They knew that their wives would hang back to let everyone out before they descended on the unsuspecting pastor.

"Well, Bob," Ben said, "it looks like a long one today. I am afraid the pastor is going to be late for dinner."

"Yep, sure looks that way. I don't know about you, Ben, but I thought she did a very good job with that solo."

"She sure did. She has a beautiful voice. But it seems as though there was more to that this morning than just the singing of a song. I can't quite put my finger on it. There was something, well, something special about the way she sang."

Ilse did not appreciate what she was hearing. "Oh sure, you men are all alike. I wouldn't expect anything different. That woman probably has all the men on her side anyway. With a reputation like hers, I wouldn't in the least be surprised if the men weren't silently applauding her."

Now it was Ben's turn to be displeased. "Ilse, that's not fair. I do not like having my faithfulness questioned like that. I just think you are making more of this than you ought. Her solo was fitting, her voice was pleasant, and I found that moment to be devotional, not like when that old warbler on the choir sings."

Bob snickered in agreement.

"But Ben," Alexis added, "you know who she is. Doesn't that count for something? Should we just throw open the doors of the church and let her and the people like her just come in and take over?"

"Alexis, don't you think you are exaggerating?" said Bob, coming to Ben's defense. "First of all, if there are many people who are thinking the way you two are, who would want to be a part of this congregation? But besides this, I don't think we have any right to stand in judgment."

The line of departing parishioners was moving more rapidly. Behind them the sexton was picking up papers and bulletins that worshipers left behind. The Altar Guild had removed the flowers from the chancel, and two members of the choir were carrying the anthem binders to the choir room.

They were now within earshot of the pastor, who was greeting his parishioners.

"Morning, pastor. Good sermon."

"I enjoyed your service this morning, pastor."

"Thank you for stopping by to see father at the hospital. Your visit meant a lot to him."

"Don't you think we sang the hymns too fast today, and can't you get the organist to play a little softer? And, by the way, was the sound system turned on today? I didn't hear a word the lector said."

Graciously the pastor thanked those who complimented him and tried to appease those who had complaints. He had a smile and a warm greeting for everyone.

And now Ilse and Alexis faced pastor McNeal. He extended his hand but neither offered to take it. Ben reached around his wife and shook the pastor's hand. "Good Morning, pastor. I better warn you. Our wives here are loaded for bear."

A look of concern clouded the cleric's face. "Oh, what is the concern?"

Alexis shot the first volley. "Come now, pastor. You don't think you could get away with what happened this morning without someone being upset."

Ilse nodded in agreement. "If no one else mentioned it, we will. We will not let this pass."

"Please, tell me. If there is anything I can do to take care of your concern, I will. You know that, don't you?"

Ilse responded, "Well, we'll see. I just can't believe that no one else in this church today complained about the solo while we were receiving communion. It was disgraceful."

"I'm sorry, I don't understand. My impression was that it was well done and quite appropriate. What was it that bothers you?"

Now it was Alexis' turn. "Pastor, don't you know who that woman is who sang that solo? Or, better yet, don't you know what sort of person she is? I thought everyone knew her reputation."

Pastor McNeal's eyes showed a deep sense of sadness. His shoulders sagged as he drew a deep breath. "Yes, I know Mary very well, and I know what sort of person she is—was. I have been working with her for a number of months now. You see, Mary was abandoned by her mother when she was a child. She was raised in foster homes. Some were good; some were not.

"All through her life she wondered about her mother, the one who gave birth to her. Almost a year ago she discovered that her mother was still alive, living in the County Home for the indigent.

"Mary went to visit her mother and heard the circumstances behind what happened. That is not important to you. But what you should know is that Mary took her mother home with her, cared for her, nursed her. Two weeks ago Mary's mother died and we had a funeral service for her. No one else was there. It was just Mary and me. Even the funeral director left the room.

"Last week Mary came to me. She knew what kind of a life she led. She confessed it and when she heard that God was not only willing to forgive her, but, through his grace and the gift of Jesus Christ, did forgive her, she repented. Mary has changed. She has found a new life. The love she discovered in her love for her mother, and the faith given by a loving and merciful God has given her a new lease on life.

"To celebrate this new life and as a gift of love to God she asked to be able to sing that solo. We could not refuse. Did you hear the words she sang? 'O love that will not let me go; I rest my weary soul on thee...' That was not just a solo. That was the offering of a precious gift to one who loves her so much that he would not give up until she was found. I am sorry you are offended. I pray you will find room in your own heart to welcome this new child into our family."

Ben and Bob stood with their hands clasped behind their backs and stared at their shoes.

Ilse and Alexis were silent. Were they scolded, or were they informed? They were not sure. Something of their own sin pointed a finger at them, yet their pride would not allow complete surrender. Ilse cleared her throat. "Well, we'll see. It will be hard to forget. Maybe she'll be different. Maybe she won't. I just don't think it was right. But if you didn't mind her singing, I guess I can overlook it."

"We have to trust your judgment," Alexis added. "Sometimes we don't agree and we have to let you know. Good day, pastor." They both walked out of the door and turned toward the parking lot.

Ben and Robert shook hands with their pastor. All they could do was shrug their shoulders. Bob muttered "Sorry."

Pastor McNeal smiled a sad smile, wondering at how hard it is for some people to forgive and love.

He turned and faced Mary. They embraced as they both gave thanks to God and offered their gift of tears.

"Those without sin may cast the first stone." You have said this, my Lord and Savior, and I have often spoken it. But I have not always practiced it. It is so simple to sit in the seat of judgment and magnify the faults of others while trying to hide or deny my own. "What right does he

have...?" "Why should she be permitted to...?" Yet, when I am in your presence, when my gaze is lifted up to your death on the cross, or when I am confronted by Scripture, or when you enter me through the Holy Eucharist, I am so mindful of my own unworth and how much I deserve judgment. Forgive me my short-sightedness and fill my heart with love and compassion and a burning desire to embrace all people and not exclude them. Amen.

How the Christmas Star Got Its Light

Theme: Christmas
Scripture: general
Season: Christmas (ABC cycles)

In the beginning, God created the heavens and the earth. And God said, "Let there be stars in the heavens."

Suddenly, there was the sound of a mighty wind. It blew and twisted and turned, gathering up all the particles and pieces floating around in the void of the universe. The pieces collided in the fierce maelstrom. When the wind ceased, dark masses hung cold and lifeless in the silent emptiness.

When all was quiet, God looked at what had been made. He was pleased to see so many stars, more than anyone could number. But, something was not right. The universe was still unfriendly, frozen, empty. God thought and thought but could not put his finger on what seemed to be missing.

"This cannot be," the Lord said. "Everything else that has been created is good. I have said so. I want the stars to be good, too. What's wrong?"

After what seemed to be an eternity, the creator called together the heavenly host—all of those who had been there from the beginning, the myriad company of angels and cherubim and seraphim. The Lord announced to them, "The stars have been created and hang in their places, but I am not yet pleased. It is not good, but I cannot recognize the problem. What is it? Can you understand?"

An uneasy rustling agitated the heavenly host. This had never happened before. God always knew what to do and had never asked for their opinion. Many of them feared making a suggestion. How would the Lord react? Would they be punished, or, worse, banished?

Just then, a strange sound was heard. It came so unexpectedly that the heavenly assembly immediately fell silent. It was the sound of someone try to call attention to himself.

All eyes turned to the front and a gasp of disbelief rose from the throng of angels. There, in front of the mighty throne of God, stood a tiny cherub, and a very young one, at that.

"Please, sir," the cherub said in a voice that quavered nervously, "I think I know what is wrong."

An amused smile curled the lips of the Father and an eyebrow arched upward and God said, "Oh, you do, do you?"

The angels and archangels could not contain themselves. They broke out in laughter and shook their wingtips at the tiny creature who was now blushing deeply.

The Lord held up a hand and silence again descended over the heavenly company. "No," said God, "we must not laugh. No one else has offered a solution. So, let us hear what the little one has to say. Tell us, little one, what must be done so that I can say that the stars are good?"

The cherub cleared its throat and started to speak. The voice was so soft that it was almost a whisper and everyone had to strain to hear it. "Kind sir," said the cherub, "it is true that you made the stars just as you made everything else, and there are so many of them that no one could count them, but, but, no one can see them."

It seemed as if all the heavenly beings had stopped breathing.

All eyes turned toward the heavens. The cherub was right! The stars could not be seen. The void looked as empty as it had been before the Lord had made the stars.

"That's it!" God shouted as he bounded from his throne, "The stars need to shine. And I know what I will do. Each star shall get a cherub to give it an inner light that will glow against the void. All you cherubim, get ready to make the stars shine. But not you, my little one. You shall not have a star. Now, the rest of you, be off!"

With a wave of God's hand the cherubim flew to the stars and became their light. The heavens began to twinkle as star after star lit up. The sight was so magnificent that even the eyes of the creator filled with wonder. Then God said, "It is good," and the heavenly host sang in praise.

All of heaven was filled with joy—except for the little cherub.

"Why can't I have a star?" he cried to himself. No one noticed as the tiny one stole silently away.

Well, the stars continued to shine. Every night now, the velvet sky of night is adorned with necklaces of light that sparkle like diamonds. Humanity has praised their beauty and pondered their mysterious light.

As years passed after the beginning, people grew more and more fascinated with the stars. They saw in them different forms and shapes. They noticed that some stars kept a constant vigil while others stayed for a season before they disappeared to return again after a period of time.

The stars shone upon the good times and the bad. They witnessed war and peace, love and hate, joy and sorrow, life and death. The years passed and a great famine fell upon the earth and its peoples—not a famine of food but of the word of God.

In time past, God had called his people to fidelity. First there had been a flood. Then an old man and his wife started a new nation. The people of this nation swung between faithfulness and disobedience. Slavery and exile reminded them of the God who had created them, but times of peace and prosperity made them forget.

The creation that God had pronounced good was now not so good as people withdrew from the Lord. Sadness gripped God's heart. He loved his people, he loved his whole creation; but all was not well. There was only one thing to do. So, a call went out: the Lord wanted to see the cherub who had first pointed out why the stars could not be seen.

After a long search, the cherub was found in a remote corner of creation where it had taken up existence away from the presence of everything that was. The cherub had wanted to forget, but it could not refuse to present itself when summoned by the Lord.

"Ah, my little one," the Lord said as the cherub bowed before the holy place, "it has been a long time, hasn't it? I have a special mission for you. You were the only cherub not to get a star, and there happens to be one star that has not yet received its light. Here is what I want you to do."

And the Lord bent down to whisper in the cherub's ear. The little one smiled widely and glowed with joy at what it heard. God finished and straightened up to say, "Now, be gone!"

The cherub left in a flash and, almost instantaneously, a new star appeared in the sky, a star bigger and brighter than any other. Its light pulsated as if to say, "Follow me, follow me."

On earth, among those who studied the stars to discover their secrets, several professionals noticed the brilliant new star whose rays seemed to reach from the highest heavens right down to earth's surface. They asked each other, "Can it be? Is this the fulfillment of what has been written so many years ago?" So, they set out in pursuit of the shining beacon.

They followed the star until it came to rest over a tiny village in a small land, and the name of the village was Bethlehem. There, the little cherub glowed its brightest and shone down on a stable, bathing the earth with glorious light as the three searchers entered, knelt, and worshiped God's Son.

And God said, "It is very good!"

Oh Holy Child of Bethlehem, my heart sings with joy every time I hear the story of your birth. In that one sacred moment you, the Son of God, became like me and lived your life as one who dwelt among your brothers and sisters. You came into the world yet you were not recognized. You continue to come into our world and often the mystery remains. But every now and again I get a glimpse of that star when it rests over one in whom you live. I cannot bring you gold, frankincense, or myrrh. The only gift I have is myself. I give it to you, Lord Jesus. And may your holy light illumine my life too. Amen.

The Delegation

Theme: loss of innocence; playfulness and prayerfulness
Scripture: Matthew 9:13-15
Season: general

"Really, Dad, how could you? I mean, after all, I was so embarrassed. All of my friends were laughing at us. I wanted to run away and hide."Trish's voice cut through the thick silence that hung over the Henderson's kitchen table like the ominous mushroom cloud following an atomic explosion.

Jim Henderson, husband to Sally, father of Trish, Robby, and Nate, and the pastor of First Church in Monroeville, looked sadly at his daughter. Fearful of saying anything, he wondered inwardly, "Poor Trish. Sixteen years old but going on sixty. When did she grow so old?"

"Yeh, Dad," it was Robby's turn now, "why did you do it? You should have heard what the kids at school were saying about you, and us. Did Mom tell you I have three nights of detention because I got in a fight defending you?"

Again Jim's inner voice spoke: "Good for you Rob. By God, there's some hope for this world when a son will still go to bat for his father. But, you'll lose it, son, you'll lose it. And when you do, your world will make sure you won't find it again."

Sally sat silently, picking at the flavorless food in front of her. She rolled the cold, B-B hard peas from one side of her plate to the other. Her red, swollen eyes betrayed her day of silent suffering and hidden tears. She sighed, "We better hurry, the delegation will be here soon."

The reminder sent a cold chill through Jim. He had often heard of pastors who received visits from the Delegation. Jim envisioned the front door of the parsonage flying open to reveal a knot of people, all dressed in dark trenchcoats with the brims of their hats pulled down over their eyes, silhouetted by the light reflected by the swirling fog behind them. "I wonder if they will be wearing armbands?"

"Da-a-a-a-d," chorused Trish and Robby.

Jim looked around the table at his family: Sally, Trish, Robby, and Nate. Nate was the only one who was not a part of the wound- licking proceedings. It might be because he was only five years old. But then again it might be that molding his mashed potatoes into an obelisk was more serious business than the embarrassment Jim brought upon those whom he loved. His intention was not to cause this pain. It was innocent enough. Jim's pain was that people just didn't understand.

Sally rose to begin to clear the table. A look from Jim at Trish got her to her feet too but not without an unspoken complaint. And the doorbell rang.

Trish dropped a fork. It clattered inside the empty vegetable dish and she let out a weak yelp.

Sally took a deep breath as she looked toward the closed door. Nate looked for some gravy to pour over his model of Cleopatra's Needle.

Jim rose. "Well, I guess this is it. I better let them in before they break down the door and drag me away. I wouldn't want my children remembering me as the man the Delegation dragged away one night after supper."

Trish was about to offer another sound of protest until she felt the squeeze of her mother's hand upon her forearm.

Jim opened the door and stood to the side to allow the small procession to file into the room. All but Emma Kravits wore trenchcoats. Jim had all he could do to keep from deepening the conflict by losing control with laughter.

There were five of them: Emma Kravits, John Fielding, Henry Price, Bertha Lutz, and Fred Collins.

Jim looked at the Delegation, wondering which one was going to be the spokesperson. It had to be Fred, he guessed. John usually didn't know what was going on with anything. He just always found himself in the middle. Bertha got too excited and would end up agreeing when she started to disagree and back again. Henry was a public official in the small town and for that reason never took an official stand for fear of hurting his political aspirations. And Emma, bless her soul, couldn't look anyone square in the eyes because her eyes didn't look in the same direction simultaneously. Yes, it had to be Fred, the local sheriff.

Sally coughed slightly and took a step toward the Delegation. "May I take your coats?"

Fred wheeled in her direction. He looked as though someone said, "Stick-em-up" to him.

"No thank you, missus. This here is important business so we won't be stayin' very long. We have something to say so it just got to be said and that will be that."

Jim thought he was in an Abbott and Costello movie.

Fred pivoted again and faced Jim. "Revrund, we've got a mighty important mission. We're here representin' the people down at First Church. Might say we're a self-appointed group of concerned citizens."

All five, including Fred, started to nod their heads in agreement.

Jim started to show signs of letting go of the build-up of laughter. He thought, "My God, they all look like the small dolls in the back windows of cars I've seen around town. You go over a bump and the heads start to nod up and down."

Fred took up his narration. "So there's no use beating around the bush. I'm going to get right to the point. No use hemming and hawing."

Again Jim said silently, "Just like the overture to a musical; you've got to hear all the songs before they start the play."Fred continued to elaborate how necessary it was not to waste any time while he wasted time. But then the play began. "Things just haven't been the same since you came to town."

With that he reached inside his partially opened coat. Sally and Trish clung to one another half expecting Fred to produce brass knuckles or a billy club. Instead, when he brought his hand out, he was holding a small spiral notebook and the stub of a yellowpencil.

Fred flipped open the notebook. "The first thing that you went and done was make us shake hands with one another during the service. Revrund, we don't come to church to be friendly. We come to get religion. What does shakin' hands or passin' the peace have to do with it? We never done it before you came, and we don't see why we should do it now."

Bump. Nod, nod, nod.

Fred flipped the page. "Then, last Easter, what did we find when we came to church? Paper butterflies hangin' from everything a string could be tied to, that's what. Why, Miss Ellie hasn't been the same since. We thought she was goin' to have apoplexy or somethin' like that. Every time she starts talking about that day, her eyes glaze over, her face gets all red, and she starts to huff and puff like ol' Engine

Seventy-Nine that used to run through town. I don't know what you're tryin' to do, but we just want you to preach the pure, unadulterated Galilean Gospel and forget these other crazy ideas of your'n."

Bump. Nod, nod, nod.

"But, Revrund, nothing beats what you did yesterday."

Major bump. Nod, shake, round-and-around.

"Where in tarnation do you come off suggestin' that we should join you in looking for Puff the Magic Dragon's cave? There ain't no such critter. We don't want you talking to us like no children. We're adults and we want grown-up talk. The idea saying that Jesus wants us to play and pray. We're all too old to play. Life's too serious. Besides, what does playin' have to do with prayin' and religion?"

Bump. Nod, nod, nod.

"We don't take kindly to you sayin' that we all are like Jackie Paper. Who's he, anyway? We never heard of him. He's not even listed in the phone book. And, Revrund, where in the hell is the land of Honah-Lee? I spent all Sunday afternoon lookin' at maps. I called in to the State Police and they don't know where it is neither. Are you pullin' our leg or sumthin'?"

Jim looked from one to the other: Fred, Emma, John, Henry, Bertha, Sally, Trish. He was sad. "When do we lose our innocence?" he wondered. "They don't understand. Life is too serious for them. They are prisoners of their own kind of reality. But is it real? Wouldn't Jesus really want us to play as well as pray? Didn't he play with his disciples, the children, the Pharisees, Zachaeus, Mary and Martha?"

And then his attention turned to Nate. He thought, "He understands. He is the only one in this room that is even close to the Kingdom. Nate knows what it is all about."

Nate looked up at his Dad, smiled, and held up the paper airplane he made out of yesterday's church bulletin.

The Delegation members had said their piece and offered their final nods farewell to the Hendersons, pleased that they were able to straighten out this new preacher of theirs and convinced that with years and experience, he would come around and give up all those foolish notions of his.

But as they turned and marched out of sight all that could be heard was Jim's soft voice singing.

A dragon lives forever but not so little boys,
Painted wings and giant rings make way for other toys.
One gray night it happened,
Jackie Paper came no more
And Puff that mighty dragon,
He ceased his fearless roar
(from "Puff the Magic Dragon," words and music by Peter Yarrow and Leonard Lipton, copywrite 1963 by Pepamar Music Corp.).

Lord of the dance, you bid us pray and play; you call us to be childlike in our faith and playful with the holy and divine things you give us as gifts. Forgive us for giving up our friendships with playful dragons and imaginary friends; for being so intent on reality that we lose sight of the vision of the kingdom you set before us; for being so adult that we become immune to your gleeful power; for being so concerned about what others will think that we are blind to your rainbow-colored glory. Defend us from the influence of the Delegation. Still the nodding of our heads. And lead us to the land of Honah-Lee. Amen!

Welcome to
MIDDLETOWN
POPULATION 125,000
875 FT. ABOVE SEA LEVEL

Can This Be Home?

Theme: hospitality; welcoming exiles in our midst
Scripture: Isaiah 58:7-10
Season: Lent (5th Sunday, A cycle)

WELCOME TO MIDDLETOWN

POPULATION 125,000 ELEVATION 875 feet

Dan stared at the sign. It was not a good omen. He had pulled off of the highway to read it in hopes that his wife, Sally, would begin to get a sense of identity with their new home. But the sign was neglected. One of the supports had been broken, probably by an accident, and the paint was peeling. Weeds threatened to swallow it. He stole a quick sideways glance at Sally, who sat with her chin in her hand and her eyes misting with tears.

"Oh, honey, please don't start crying again. It hurts me so much when you do. I know you are unhappy, and I am not too thrilled with the idea myself, but there was nothing I could do."

"I'm sorry, Dan," she said as she picked a tissue from her lap.

"I just don't know why it has to be this way." She could not look at Dan. He read her so well and she knew it was not fair to put him through all of this. Still, her gaze was glued to the tips of her shoes.

"Sally, you know that I would not be doing this if I didn't have to. But, it was either this or my job. You know how difficult it is to get work these days. There aren't a lot of openings for people in my profession. I must go where the work is."

The flood gates opened, the tears flowed, and months of pent-up frustration poured out.

"I know," she shouted, "but it is not fair. Damn your company anyway. They don't give a tinker's damn about what they do to people. Do they care about the fact that my mother is ill and I am her only child? *No!* Do they care that we have a baby on the way? *No!* All they care about is what is good for business. Well, you're here, and I'm here, but it's not because I want to be."

"I understand," Dan said in a quiet voice, "and the first chance we get, we'll go back. I'm not happy about the move either and I know it will be harder for you to make the adjustment. Let's just promise that we'll do it together. It's just you, me, and little what's-his-name.

Sally had to laugh in spite of herself. Her hand involuntarily went down to her abdomen where she let it rest as if to protect the new life that was forming.

Dan started the car. "Well, what do you say we go to our new home? I do wish you would have been with me when I saw it. The company got us a nice house in a nice neighborhood. You are going to like it. You'll see. Things have to get better."

But they didn't. As soon as Dan pulled the car onto the highway, the heavily overcast sky opened and the rain fell in sheets. All they could see of Middletown on their first day were the brief glimpses when the windshield wipers cleared enough rain away for them to see out of the window.

The weather made traffic move very slowly. Though their home was not far from the town limits, the trip seemed interminable. At long last Dan made a lefthand turn and pulled into the driveway.

"Well, here we are, honey. This is home: 1735 Elm Court. Are you ready to go in, or do you want to wait a while?"

Sally shook her head. "No, I'm okay now. Dan, I'm sorry. It is not fair for me to make it harder for you. I am not doing this on purpose. I'll try. I promise! I'll try."

"I know you will, and I do understand. But I must warn you. Remember the good news, when we were told my company was going to pay for and provide moving?"

"Yes, I remember."

"And remember how we marked all of the boxes with what room all the stuff went into?"

"Um-hum."

"Well, the deal was they would put everything in the rooms. We've got to put it away."

"Are you trying to prepare me for what we will find inside?"

"You got it, kiddo!" Dan said with the grin that Sally said made him look like a little kid. "Let's go. I don't think the rain will let up any and we better not put off facing the carnage any longer."

Sally laughed as she opened the door and ran up the steps to the front door. The roof over the small porch protected her from being soaked.

Dan was right behind her and hunted on his key ring for the right key.

"Here it is," he said as he turned the key and opened the door. With that he swept Sally up in his arms and before crossing the threshold said, "It is going to be first-class all the way."

"Oh, Dan," she said laying her head on his shoulder, "I do love you very much."

It is a good thing she did because neither she nor Dan were prepared for what they found. Furniture was standing in the middle of the room and boxes were piled high and deep.

Dan looked sheepishly at Sally as he closed the door behind them. "The bad news is that this is just one of six rooms."

They stood there for a number of moments just looking at all the work before them. It was overwhelming.

"Will we ever get all this stuff put away?" Sally wondered.

"We better," Dan answered, "if we want to eat and have a place to sleep. My problem is I don't know where to begin."

"Maybe we can begin with you showing me around this place. I must admit that it does have potential. I am sure glad your company gave you a few days to help me get things straightened up."

Dan groaned at the thought of what lay before him.

Just as they started walking through the house, the doorbell rang. Dan and Sally looked at each other. "I wonder who that is," they said together.

"Our first visitors," Sally said as she walked to the front door and opened it.

It was still pouring rain. The woman who stood on the porch was dripping wet.

"Hi," she said, "my name is Margo, Margo Jenkins. We're your nextdoor neighbors. Welcome to Elm Court. We saw the moving truck here yesterday so we kind of expected that you would be arriving today. You from far away? You must be. You have an out of state license on your car. It's hard to move away from home, isn't it, honey? I know.

Cried for a week before I could get used to the idea. Well, don't you worry none. This is a nice place to live, great neighborhood, and a church down the block that has so many activities you could be out every night of the week if you wanted to. But, there is time enough for that later on. Now you have a lot of work to do, so I'll let you get to it. We're happy to see you here, and if there is anything we can do just call over the back fence. After you get yourselves settled, my husband and I will drive you around so that you can find out where the things are in this town. Well, I'll let you get to your unpacking. Oh, I almost forgot. I do forget things. Bob, my husband, and I want you over for dinner tonight. We'll eat at six."

With that she closed the door and was gone. Sally looked at Dan and was just about to say something when the door bell rang again. It was Margo.

"I'm sorry, I just don't know where my mind is today. I told you who we were but I didn't even ask you your names."

Dan smiled. "We're the Vincenti's. I'm Dan, and this is my wife, Sally."

"Pleased to meet you," Margo smiled back, "got to run. See you at six."

Once again the door closed. Sally looked at Dan and they both started to laugh. "Come on, Sally," Dan said, "let's get some work done before dinner."

Sally cocked her head to the side. "You know, Dan, if I give it a chance I might even like this place. I wonder if Bob is at all like Margo?"

Again they laughed as they opened the first box.

In the comfort of my own home, dear Lord, I am grateful for the safety, the security, and the satisfaction I enjoy. But, I do forget there are those "exiles" who are living in my community—maybe even next door—and I do not know it. I am reminded that in our midst are those who are living here though they do not want to; they are living in a strange community and among people they do not know; they live here but their hearts are far away in that place they call home. My church, that community and fellowship of believers, can be a welcoming place, a place that can take away some of the sting and the hurt of separation. I, my Lord, have the opportunity to reach out and offer hospitality to the "stranger in our midst." At one time my family were strangers in a strange land. But they were welcomed, and they made this place home. Let me not close the doors of my home to keep out the cares of the world, but inspire me to open them to those who need a neighbor, a friend, a brother or sister in Christ. Amen.

The Night **They** *Were There*

Theme: God's kingdom (a banquet); with whom will you eat?
Scripture: Matthew 18:15-20
Season: Pentecost (16th Sunday, A cycle)

It was obvious from the moment that George and Ethel entered the parish Fellowship Hall that they were not at all pleased with what they saw.

Leaning her head toward George and holding the back of her hand in front of her mouth to prevent anyone from reading her lips, Ethel whispered, "What are *they*, of all people, doing here?"

"I don't know," George muttered out of the side of his mouth, making him look as though the other side had been paralyzed, "but if this is Father Caruso's idea of a joke, it ain't funny. There's no way this is going to work."

What they saw was indeed a strange sight. There were two groups in the large room. They were separated, like two islands, by the banquet tables. On the one side, *they* clustered in small, loose groups, uneasy, uncomfortable, and very self-conscious. The little conversation that was taking place was muffled whispers. Mostly *they* just stood around looking at the floor tiles or the tops of *their* shoes.

Most of the noise came from the other group on the opposite side of the ocean of tables. This group, folks George and Ethel knew from the parish, were standing around the punch table and the hors d'oeuvres.

Miriam looked over and saw George and Ethel standing disbelievingly by the doors. She waved, took her husband, Pete, by the sleeve of his jacket, and led him to where George and Ethel were standing.

"Can you believe this?" Miriam asked. "I had no idea that *they* were invited too. It was even a surprise to Pete, wasn't it dear?"

"Damn right! I'm even on the parish council." Pete was genuinely disturbed. "It is probably going to wreck the whole evening for the lot of us. It doesn't look like *they* are enjoying themselves either, the little that I care."

Suddenly George let out a soft moan. "Oh God. Name cards. I guess this means that we are going to have to sit next to them."

Pete put his arm around his friend's shoulder. "Don't worry, Miriam and I already saw to that. We found our name tags and moved a few around so that we will be sitting together. I'm dying to tell you about my round of golf today. I hit an eagle on the 16th. You know, that long par five."

"Get out! An eagle? What did you do, carry the ball up to the pin and drop it in?"

The comic relief was welcome, for the tension in the room was thick enough to cut with a knife.

Just then Father Caruso walked into the room. He waved a friendly greeting to the *other* group of people, who smiled and nodded back to him as though to say, "What have you gotten us into?" As he made his way through the hall, he received a polite but reserved response from nearly everyone. Harry was different. Harry was always different.

"Well, Father, I've got to hand it to you. You finally found a way to get this group of people and *them* together. You've sure got chutzpah." Harry's voice echoed through the fellowship hall.

"Oh God," George groaned while he rolled his eyes. "Leave it to Harry. He'd look for a diamond ring in a pile of horse—"

"George," Ethel interrupted. "Mind yourself now."

Father Caruso called for everyone's attention. "By now you realize that we have your names on cards to designate where you will be sitting. Knowing you, you have already found your places."

A nervous laugh rippled over the two uncomfortable groups.

"I have received word that our dinner is ready, so why don't we just go and sit down."

The priest was right. The people knew where their places were. George and Ethel and Miriam and Pete went to their seats and sat down. It took them only a few seconds to realize everyone else was standing waiting for the pastor to offer a prayer. With sheepish grins that betrayed embarrassment, they stood making a loud noise as their chairs scraped against the linoleum floor.

Father Caruso invited everyone to bow their heads. "Father, for the blessings we are about to receive and the work of your Holy Spirit, we give you thanks. Amen."

A wave of "Amens" lapped over the long table.

Doors swung open and the "Kitchen Krew" began wheeling in carts loaded with steaming hot food.

George looked up and down the table and noticed that *they* were all on the other side of the table, while the people he was familiar with were all on his side. He noticed something else. The potatoes and vegetables were all being set on his side of the table and the meat and gravy on *their* side; relish dishes and bread plates graced the center.

"Before we start eating, I want to share something with you." Father Caruso remained seated while he spoke. "First, I want to apologize if I made any of you feel unduly uncomfortable. I was watching you from the other side of those doors," he pointed behind him, "and I was not surprised at what I saw; no, even moving the place cards was not a surprise."

Pete winked at Ethel and George and smiled a boyish smile.

The cleric continued, "I invited all of you, and for a reason. You may not agree or understand, but I do hope you will keep an open mind."

"I heard a story some time ago that I would like to share with you. This person died and was met in the great heavenly kingdom by St. Peter. 'Let me show you around,' St. Peter said. They came to a room in which a banquet was taking place. On the table was a feast that topped all feasts. But no one was happy. Everyone in the room had a three-foot spoon tied to his or her arm and when they tried to eat they could not bring the food to their mouths."

"'Interesting,'" said the newcomer.

"'Yes,'" replied St. Peter. "'This is hell.'"

"They went up one step and came to another room. A banquet was being held there too. The tables nearly buckled under the weight of the food. And the people there also had three-foot spoons tied to their arms. But they were happy; they were feeding one another.

"'I know,'" said the visitor, "'this is heaven.'"

The priest paused. "Tonight can either be a taste of heaven or hell. You can eat what is on your side of the table or you can share it by passing it across. If you share I do want you to introduce yourself and learn something about the person sitting across from you."

At first it was awkward. But it wasn't too long before people were actually looking at one another across the table—and talking. George met a lovely young woman with deep, dark eyes. Her name was Carla, and surprise of surprises, they worked in the same building. He discovered that she was going to night school in order to move out of the secretarial pool.

The dinner progressed well. All the food was eaten, and the air was filled with conversation and even laughter. George didn't even mind when Harry yelled down to him, "Hey George, this guy here has a small orchestra. You're looking for one for the parish social, aren't you? Talk to him afterwards."

All in all the evening was a success. A few new friendships were established. A couple made arrangements to get together again. George and Ethel invited Carla and her family to come to church with them on Sunday and were surprised when they agreed. "Great," George said. "Suppose we pick you up. After church we'll grab a brunch down at the hotel, my treat." It was a date.

Oh, not everyone left pleased. There were some who vowed not to be a part of anything like this again. Two couples made up their minds to attend another neighboring parish.

As the crowd began to filter out, Father Caruso was standing next to George. "Well, Father," George said, "I would not have bet on it when I came in, but it looks like you pulled something off here tonight."

"Think so, George?"

"Yeh, I do. I must be honest, I never thought I would be comfortable around *them*. Tonight was an education. *They* are okay. Think we can do this again?"

"I hope so, George. George, do you think that it will ever happen?

"What do you mean?"

"Do you think there will ever come a time when the word *they* will become *us*?

You told us, Lord, that the Kingdom of Heaven is like a banquet, a feast, a party. That sounds good! But, who else will be there? With whom will I be eating? Will I stay away because of who is there? The Pharisees did that. They stayed outside and grumbled while the party went on inside. Not only that, Lord; why do I use language that separates instead of unites? I have so much to learn; so much accepting to do; so much loving to offer. But I want to do it. I don't want to be standing outside the door. I like parties, and I want to be at yours. Amen.

Her Master's Voice

Theme: listening to (for) God's voice
Scripture: John 10:1-10
Season: Easter (4th Sunday, A cycle)

"M*other!*" Jennifer's complaining voice carried from the living room to the kitchen. "Mother, she's doing it again!"

"Oh dear," Sandra said barely audibly for herself to hear. She dried her hands on her apron.

"Oh dear," she repeated. "Oh dear."

"I'll be right there, honey," she called out to her daughter. But Jennifer didn't wait. She stormed into the kitchen, throwing the swinging door open so violently that it creaked as it strained against its aging spring-loaded hinges.

"Really, mother, you are going to have to do something about Grandma. She's ruining my life. It's, like, totally weird."

Sandra silently made a wish that she would be able to understand what Jennifer was saying. She was finding out that words don't always mean the same today that they did years ago.

"She just sits in her rocking chair and talks. She talks and talks, but no one is there. Mother, just now, she was carrying on a conversation. Really now, even you must think that is a little strange."

Sandra's heart was heavy. She knew it was hard on Jennifer. But this was her mother.

"I can't even have my friends over. When they do come, some giggle at grandma and others sit and mock her. Yesterday, in school, Denise, my very best friend, asked me how things were in the Twilight Zone."

"Jen, honey," Sandra was finally able to interject, "I know this is hard on you. But, please try to understand. This is my mother. She's old, and tired, and lonely. Ever since your grandfather died, she has missed him so. They were married for nearly sixty years. That's a long time to be together."

Jennifer pouted. "Oh, I know. But it just isn't fair. Don't you care about me?"

"Of course I do. I care very much. But grandma won't be with us much longer. You know her health is failing. I want to make her remaining time as comfortable as possible and for her to be with the people she loves—and who love her even if her conversations with no one are unsettling. But, I'll see what I can do. I'll go and talk with her."

"A lot of good that's going to do," Jennifer said as she sulked out of the kitchen. "I'm going up to my room."

Jennifer punctuated her anger and frustration with each step on the stairs, with the final exclamation given with the slamming of her door.

A dark sadness enshrouded Sandra as she made her way to the living room.

There, rocking and smiling contentedly, sat her mother: a small, frail, benign woman who hummed as she rocked.

Seeing Sandra she stopped the motion of her chair.

"Hello, dear. Did you come to pay me a visit? I am afraid you caught me without anything prepared to give you. Maybe I can find some cookies in the kitchen. I'll brew us a pot of tea."

She made to get up from her chair. Sandra interrupted. "No, that's okay, mother. I didn't come to visit you. You live with us now, remember?"

A doubtful look crossed her mother's face. "Do I? I'm so sorry. I seem to forget these things. My memory is not like it used to be."

"That's all right, mother. Besides, you remember things from long ago. I like when you tell me about those times."

"You do, dear? Well, it just so happened that I was just thinking about—"

"Not now, mother. Jennifer tells me you were talking to yourself again."

"Jennifer?"

"Your granddaughter."

"Oh, yes. What a fine girl she is. Reminds me a lot of you when you were her age."

"Mother, the talking."

"Sandra, I just had the nicest visit. We talked and he made me feel so good."

"Please, mother, daddy died years ago. You can't talk to him. Please try to understand how hard this is on all of us."

"I wasn't talking to your father, Sandra."

"You weren't? Well, who then?"

"I was talking with Jesus. He was so nice. He told me I shouldn't be afraid. He told me that there will be a place for me when he comes for me. His voice was so soft and warm."

Sandra felt that she was losing her patience. "Mother, this has got to stop. Besides, how do you know it was Jesus? Did you see him?"

"Goodness no! I didn't see him. I knew it was Jesus by his voice."

Sandra threw up her hands. "I give up. Mother, please try not to be difficult. You are talking to your imagination and it is hard on the rest of the family. Please try to remember."

Well, no one slept well that night. Jennifer's anger continued to eat at her late into the night. Sandra hurt because of the difficulty her daughter was facing and because of her mother's progressive separation from reality. Sandra missed her husband and wished he would soon return from his business trip. They would have to make a decision about her mother.

Even the dog's night was restless, having some sense of tension and strange happenings.

When morning came, Jennifer found her mother in the kitchen, sitting at the table, staring into a cup of coffee. Her face showed signs of crying.

"Mother, what's wrong? Are you all right?"

"Come over here and sit down with me. Grandma's not with us anymore."

"What do you mean? What happened?"

"She died in her sleep last night."

"Oh mother, I am so sorry. I feel so ashamed."

"No, don't. Don't blame yourself. Don't feel sorry. Her death was calm and peaceful. She had the sweetest smile on her face when I found her this morning. She is at peace, and with the ones she wants to be with."

"But it's so sudden. We didn't know. She wasn't strong but she wasn't sick either."

"No, we didn't know, but I think grandma did. You see, honey, yesterday afternoon, when she was talking, she had a very special visitor. She heard his voice; she knew who he was; and now she is with him."

"Speak, Lord, for your servant listens." But, I do not always stay still or quiet long enough to hear you. Perhaps I

am afraid to hear your voice. You know what they say about people to claim to hear you speaking! I am not sure I want to risk that. And, when I wake up in the middle of the night and can't sleep, I concentrate more on trying to get back to sleep than to listen to hear what you may have called me for. There have been times, many times, that I longed to hear your voice just to know that I am not in this alone. I do believe that you do speak to me. I also believe that I have not heard because I have not been listening. Slow me down, Lord. Help me to feel comfortable with silence. Come to me as that still small voice. Speak, Lord, for your servant is listening. Amen.

What Is One to Do?

Theme: doing the right thing
Scripture: Luke 10:38-42
Season: Pentecost (8th Sunday, C cycle)

It was moments like these that made Millie nervous. She had been warned that things like this would happen when she accepted the job. And they did. She never got used to it.

Millie liked her job at St. Jude's parish. It was a Godsend. When Larry died so suddenly, she was at wit's end worrying about how she was going to make ends meet. She had to work. The kids deserved a chance to go to college. In the meantime, the bills had to be paid and food purchased.

The position for parish secretary opened just at the right time. Millie was hired the same day as her interview. It was during the time of orientation that she learned of these moments.

St. Jude was located on a busy thoroughfare. The street that passed in front of the church was the main artery through town. It was, therefore, an easy target for every panhandler passing by. Hardly a week went by without at least one person with a hard-luck story stopping at the office to ask for money for bus fare, gas, lodging, and every other conceivable reason under the sun. Millie found herself grading the people on the originality of their story.

Well, she had been told that when these situations arose, there were procedures to be followed. The Council of Churches had targeted and printed a list of all of the social service agencies in the area. St. Jude's parish council had the list laminated for easy reference. The council was also quite firm that since there were agencies to care for these persons, the secretary should waste no time in making the proper referral. The long and short of it was, the council wanted the people out of the building as quickly as possible.

So, what to do was clearly defined for Millie. Yet, she was not always sure. Once in a while, the story got to her and her heart went out to the person. She wanted to help too, to do a little more than be a clearing house for the agencies. Sometimes it was just too impersonal. And she also wasn't sure that the needs of the people were really being met. Millie believed that caring for people was more than handing out food, money, or tickets for a place to stay for the night. Issues such as loneliness, homelessness, fear, and injustice were not being addressed.

Still, Millie was always ill at ease. She knew what she had to do; there it was in black and white, preserved between two sheets of plastic, but she often did not do what she wanted to do.

This time the man who sat next to her desk surfaced those feelings of anxiety and frustration. His face was that of a sad person, etched deeply with the lines of loneliness and need. His eyes, though gentle, had lost their luster. Millie sensed a feeling of uneasiness. He was apologetic. He was also vulnerable. Millie was afraid for him.She opened the top drawer of her desk. There, in a place cleared specially for it, was the laminated procedure. Millie knew what she had to do. It was spelled out carefully. All it took was a phone call to the right agency, the referral, and the stranger would be on his way.

She pushed the drawer closed with forceful determination. "Not this time," she said to herself. "He is not going to get lost in a bureaucratic shuffle. I know what I am supposed to do. But, just maybe, just this once, I can do a little more."

Millie pushed the intercom button that rang in the pastor's office. "Pastor, two weeks ago you shared with us during the staff meeting that there is a member of this church that has a live-in job for someone who is handy. Do you know if that position is still available? It is? Good, I think I have someone who might fill that bill. Does he have any qualifications? Would you believe a woman's intuition?" She looked up and smiled at the stranger. Lifeless eyes now danced and sparkled.

As she spoke Millie remembered her conversation with the drop-in. It was strange. He didn't ask for money. He wasn't just passing through; he didn't have a sick wife in the car; there weren't any children held by an agency in another town. He was alone; he had lost everything in a fire. His wife left him a couple of years back for another man. The pain remembered sent a shudder through his thin body. He wasn't even sure why he came into St. Jude's. Probably a desperate attempt to find out if there was anyone who really cared.

She went back to her conversation with the pastor. "I know that this is irregular. Yes, I also know that I am not going through the proper channels and that I am not doing things right. Can you trust me on this one? Something tells me that this is the right thing. Thank you very much. I am sure that this will work out just fine." She placed the phone on its cradle. "Well, I think that this is just what the doctor ordered. It will give you a chance to get on your feet, become established, and move on to something better when things improve. Have you eaten recently?"

The man shook his head. "Not for some time."

"Well, it's lunch time. I am famished and you must be starved too. I want to take you out for lunch if you don't mind a fast- food burger."

He smiled. "Not at all. I will be happy to join you if you will let me take you to lunch some day."

"It would be my pleasure."

Millie locked up all that was supposed to be secured when the office was empty. She almost laughed when she realized that this was perhaps the only procedure she followed correctly that morning. "Oh well," she thought, "I did do the right thing. Besides what else could I do? He is my neighbor, isn't he?"

All my life, Lord, I have been taught to do things right. And that is good, I guess. Otherwise all I would have is a lame excuse for sloppy work. But, in reading your word I have also learned that it is important to do the right thing. The dilemma is that sometimes I must choose between doing things right and doing the right thing. That's when I need you, Lord. I don't want to pass by the person in need because I must be at a meeting or because I have duties in the church or because my agenda for the day will get all messed up. Is it true that my neighbor is that person for whom I should sacrifice doing things right in order to do the right thing? The decision is not always easy to make nor are the areas clearly defined. I know I must make the decisions. But, Lord, I pray for your wisdom and courage to know the difference between my neighbors need and my agenda, between established guidelines and the cry for help. Amen.

One Cold and Windy Day

Theme: encountering the living Christ
Scripture: Luke 16:19-31
Season: Pentecost (24th Sunday, C cycle)

A ragged man huddled in the corner of the bank entrance to find shelter from the cold winter wind. Jim tried to avoid looking into his eyes as he walked by. The homeless people in town were growing in numbers.

Jim and the other members of the Chamber of Commerce did not know what to do with them. They were an embarrassment, a nuisance, and bad for business. Yet, they were there, obviously present. So, since they would not go away, the least the Chamber of Commerce could do was sponsor a soup kitchen where these poor souls could get at least one good meal a day.

Besides, their "charitable compassion," well covered in the local newspaper, was good publicity. What with the proliferation of suburban malls, the downtown merchants could use all the help they could get.

But Jim was not at all pleased this day. He just could not understand why he had to go to the church basement where the soup kitchen was housed to help serve the meal. "Isn't it enough we support this with our contributions?" he argued with himself. "Why must I take the time away from my business to do this?"

The truth is, Jim had been able to get out of it every time his name came up to serve. He had an excuse, and the others were always able to cover for him. That was not the case this time, however. His fellow members of the Chamber, seeing through his excuses, said it was time for him to make his appearance. Jim's reticence was no secret. Jim picked up his pace. Hope Church was just a block away. "The sooner I get there, I can get this over with." He did not have to finish. He knew how he felt.

The room where the meal was served was spartan but warm and friendly. The clatter of dishes and pots from the kitchen mingled with the din raised by those who had gathered. It was obvious that a camaraderie among the "guests" had evolved. Almost everyone was talking about the freezing wind.

"Hi, Jim! Glad you could make it." It was Pete Reynolds, the president of the Chamber of Commerce.

"Yeah, yeah," Jim complained as he hung his coat on a hook. His imported wool topcoat stood out among the older coats that surrounded it. "Can we start soon? I've got a lot to do today."

"We're just about ready, Jim. Be patient. Here, you better wear this apron. You're going to help serve."

"Oh great. Don't you have a chef's hat so that I can look completely ridiculous?"

Pete turned to the others in the kitchen. "Can't you tell that Jim is just bubbling with joy over being here today?"

They all laughed. Everyone, that is, except Jim.

"All right, folks, we're about ready to start serving, so you better find a place to sit." The voice was strong and husky. Jim recognized it. "That's Margaret what's-her-name, one of the lead singers for our town's musical theater," he observed silently. Paying more attention to the workers, he recognized others: the vice-president of the town council, the chief of police, and there, giving a slight wave of greeting, Pastor Williams, the rector of Jim's church.

The people moved quickly to the tables and found places to sit. Quite suddenly, the tumult gave way to silence with a few coughs and sniffles. Then, at the center table, a man stood. All eyes turned to him. Jim had never seen him before but others seemed to know him well.

He cleared his throat. "Let us pray." At the invitation, hands folded and heads bowed, except Jim's. He was stunned. "What's going on?" he wondered.

"Loving Father," the man continued, "sometimes, it appears that we don't have too much to call our own. But today we see how blessed we are. We have these friends who have come to feed us; we have this warm place out of the cold; we have the bounty of your hands in the food we will eat; we have one another; but most of all we are blessed because you are with us. Bless those whose hands prepared this meal, those who gave the food, and especially those who love us enough to provide this time and place. May this be a foretaste of the feast that is to come, the banquet that awaits us all in your kingdom of glory. Amen."

"Amen," the people chorused.

With that, the serving carts were wheeled out. Steam rose from the hot food, and words of satisfaction and appreciation filled the air.

Jim blinked. He did not know what happened, but a warm feeling enveloped him. He quickly took off his apron and threw it on the countertop, rushed over to where his coat hung, and hastily put it on. Not bothering to button it, he ran toward the stairs.

"Where are you going, Jim? We need you to help serve."

Jim did not answer or look back. He took the steps two at a time. "Oh, God, I hope I'm not too late. Please, God, don't let me be too late."

Finally he stopped. A smile beamed on his face. "Thank God," he said out loud.

Jim stepped forward and extended his hand to the man who was still huddled in the bank entrance.

"Come, my friend, let's go where there's some food to feed you and friends to welcome you."

Lord God, Yahweh, you know that I am always in a hurry, bustling hither and yon on errands that I feel are of vital importance. But when I do, I am not aware of the need that is surrounding me. I do not see the faces of the homeless, the cold, and the hungry. I do not sense the tears of the lonely, the forgotten, and the unhappy. I do not hear the silent screaming of those whose roots have been torn out of the ground called home and forced to be transplanted in a place that is feared. There are times, I confess, that it is not that I miss them; I just don't want to be bothered. You, however, did not pass any by. You gave sight to the blind who called out from the roadside. You paused at a well and brought salvation to a woman who was part of a despised race. You were the bubbling water at the Pool of Bethesda for a lame man. I want to be this kind of a friend to those I encounter. Help me to learn. Teach me your compassion. Fill me with your love. Amen.

First Light

Theme: God's laughter; resurrection (Easter)
Scripture: Matthew 28:1-10; Mark 16:1-8; Luke 24:1-11
Season: Easter (ABC cycles)

A blanket of peace covered the slumbering city. The sky above, still adorned with the sparkling jewels of light, was washed with the deep purple of night. The first hints of twilight had not yet begun to erase the darkness along the eastern horizon.

Just a few creatures were starting to stir. Here and there, housecats were returning home from their nightly forage in the fields outside the city's walls. Stray dogs lazily opened their eyes to watch the returning felines but did not consider leaving the warmth of the place where they lay worth the fun of the chase. And, anticipating that the time was near, cocks, still perched on their roosts, stretched their wings, ruffled their feathers, and faced east to await the signal that the time to sound the call had come. The foolish ones believed that it was their cry that made the bright light shine in the sky. But the wisest knew that their herald was to call all creation to pay homage to the One who pushed back the covers of night and filled the earth with His light.

In the poorer section of the city, known as Jerusalem, a small group of women silently stole out of the house in which they were staying, being careful not to wake the sleeping men. They carried in their arms the elements of the task that caused them to arise so early: linen, spices, oils, and ointments, all of which were needed to prepare a body for burial. Wordlessly they made their way along the narrow street, pulling their cloaks close to their bodies to ward off the chill of the early morning air. Though their purpose for being up was grim and unpleasant, they resolutely headed toward the garden in which the body of their loved one had lain through the whole previous day. They had been prevented from completing these preparations because the previous day was the Sabbath.

In the garden that contained a wall of solid rock honeycombed with caves for burial, a Roman centurion stood guard while his comrades nodded off because of their boring detail. Only in this god-forsaken place would Caesar's elite be required to guard a grave. And the reason for doing it was equally ludicrous: to make sure no one would steal the body. The entrance to the sepulcher in question was covered by a large, round millstone sealed to prevent any tampering with it.

In a grove of olive and palm trees opposite the tomb, a dark featureless figure remained undetected as it leaned against the trunk of one of the trees. It kept vigil all through the night, never wavering its penetrating stare from the gravesite. It seemed to be waiting for something, but what? What could possibly happen in a cemetery?

It started as a slight vibration of the earth. The guard, detecting the movement, drew his sword and stood ready to remain loyal to his command. The figure in the grove of trees became erect and alert as though recognizing a signal announcing that danger was near. The vibration became a violent tremor. All of the Roman guards were alert but filled with fear. Two soldiers fled with hopes of finding safer ground. The one who had been awake was thrown off his feet and when he landed he quickly covered his head to protect himself from anything that might fall on it. The mysterious figure held on to the tree to keep from falling.

Slowly but deliberately, the round stone that covered the opening of the grave started to roll away revealing a large, open, gaping, black hole in the side of the hill. The trembling of the earth ceased and all was still once again.

The soldiers were paralyzed with fear and kept their eyes averted from the open tomb. The furtive shadow among the trees remained riveted to its spot, but its hollow burning eyes refused to waver from the open wound in the rock that contained the putrid decaying flesh of death.

At first it was but a faint pinpoint of light. Its glow could hardly be detected and could have been mistaken for the glow of a firefly. But without warning the glow exploded with the brilliance of a thousand suns sending a blinding ray of light skyward to meet the first ray of dawn. The light of heaven and the light of earth were joined as one. And seeing the first light, the cocks announced the birth of a new day.

Inside the cave the figure of a man was seen to arise from the stone table on which he had been lying. Slowly, bathed in the brilliance of the light that emanated from deep within, he walked to the entrance of the tomb. He stopped and looked into the shadows of the grove, his eyes locking on the sulking figure.

He recognized the one who had been covered by the darkness of the grove. He had seen him many times: in the wilderness, in cities, in crowds, among his friends. He had been there. No one else had seen the creature, but he had. Oh, yes, he knew him well.

He beckoned for the shadow to come forward and waited until he was able to look squarely into the eyes of his adversary.

"We meet again."

The figure nodded in agreement.

"Do you remember when you tried to get me to turn stones into bread to satisfy my hunger; to throw myself off a high place to prove my Father's love for me; to worship you in order to gain the kingdoms of the world?"

Again, all the figure could do was nod.

"This, foe of mine, is your final moment. You shall hunger for the souls of people as I hungered for bread, but you shall not be satisfied. You have sought to lift yourself up, but this day you have fallen. You desired to be worshipped as a god, but today you are driven to your knees before the Lord God Yahweh. You have lost the battle, Satan. Never again shall we meet, for you will be cast into outer darkness. You have seen the light of glory for the last time. You have not won. You have been vanquished. Be gone, Prince of Evil. You have sought to do your worst, but my Father has turned it into grace. Leave and inhabit the region of emptiness."

The crouching figure convulsed and blew the last of its fetid breath at the one whom he tried to defeat, the one whom he sought to own. And then, it was gone.

At that moment the vaults of heaven rang with the laughter of God. The joke was on Satan. His Son, once dead, is now alive. And the dawn glowed with the first light of a new life. Once again order was brought out of chaos and all of creation was in harmony. The day of resurrection had dawned and the women arrived to find that life had conquered death and their sadness was turned to joy; their doubts to certainty; and their disappointment to faith. Christ is risen. He is risen indeed!

Crucified Lord and risen Redeemer, with the first light of dawn on that new day, the very chains of death were broken and the reign of the evil one was brought to an end. You have life so that all of your brothers and sisters in the family of humanity may also have life. This is your will. This is your joyous surprise on the day of the Resurrection. On that day your Father laughed because the prevailing powers of sin had done their worst, and it was not enough. Sin was brought to its knees and your Holy Good triumphed over evil. Therefore, with a heart filled with joy and gladness, I can proclaim with all of my brothers and sisters in Christ: "Christ is risen! He is risen indeed!" Amen.

Unless I See

Theme: faith; grace; salvation
Scripture: John 20:19-31
Season: Easter (2nd Sunday, ABC cycles)

"HELP...Help...help...elp...elp!" the distress call caromed off of the sheer hostile walls of the cliffs of granite until the mournful echo silently died in the far distance.

"Can anybody hear ME...Me...me...e...e?"

But the only replies to be heard were the eerie moan of the cold wind and the shrill shrieks of the eagles that had built their aeries high in the mountains.

On a small ledge formed by an outcropping of the rock face of the mountain, lay the body of the distressed person twisted and racked with pain from the fall. His left leg jutted out at an unnatural angle; cuts and bruises covered his body. Almost with regularity he slipped in and out of consciousness, and he knew enough to realize that the final effect of shock was not too far away.

"Climbing the face of this mountain alone was a dumb thing to do," his inner voice scolded. He knew that. He didn't need that pesty companion to remind him of his foolishness. But he had done it before, many times before. He thought he knew the mountain well. But all it took was one misstep, the giving way of his foothold, and here he was, helpless, and, if someone didn't come soon, near death.

"Lucky for you that this ledge was here," his mental companion told him. Or was he lucky? Which is a better way to die, all at once or a little at a time?

He tried to shake the thoughts of death from his mind. "I must keep a positive outlook," he reminded himself, "or I'm done for."

It was starting to get darker. "Why is it getting dark? It must only be close to noon." He then realized that he was about to slip into unconsciousness again. "Don't worry," his inner voice soothed, "it's nature's way of providing relief from your pain."

But that was no consolation. With a burst of desperation he called out again, "Help!" but it was little more than a whisper. It was then that he noticed the figure of a man kneeling by his side. It was hard to determine his age, and he was dressed strangely, much like a hermit. He had heard of folks like these living in the mountains, but he had never encountered one before. Was he real or was this one of the hallucinations that accompany shock?

The figure bent closer as if to listen for breathing or look for signs of life.

"Yes, I'm alive," the words screamed in his brain, "do something! Go get help. I don't know how long I can hold on any more."

He felt warm hands resting on his brow. The stranger's head was tilted back and he was looking heavenward as though in prayer.

"Oh great, he's giving up on me too, probably praying my soul into its eternal rest."

But, suddenly his whole body convulsed as though hit by a powerful electrical jolt. A hot flash shot through his limbs, terminating at the tips of his fingers and toes. His leg, which had resembled that of a rag doll, was now straight. Though the pain was still there, it had subsided to be somewhat tolerable.

As his vision cleared, he realized he was looking into the face of his rescuer. It was a gentle face. The lips curled up in a kind smile.

"Welcome back," the hermit said. "I wasn't sure I got here in time. It looks as though you were quite fortunate. But why—?"

"Please," came the reply from the injured as he weakly held up his hand to stop the question, "please don't ask me why I was out here by myself. I've been asking myself that question ever since I landed here."

The questioner stopped with a nod and a broader smile. "Do you think you can stand? Here, give me your hand and we'll see what we can do."

"But my leg—"

"Give it a try. I think you'll find that it is okay. You may have a lot of pain in it, but it will hold your weight."

The hermit took his hands and helped him to his feet.

"Whoa," the injured man said as he was hit with vertigo and reached out for support.

"Take it easy. Here, put your arm over my shoulder and let me be your support. Let's try a few steps to see that everything is working properly."

The steps were hesitant and pain accompanied each one. But with clenched teeth and determination, they were soon walking with reasonable agility.

"You're doing fine. I think we will be able to make it now. You let me help you and we'll get you off this ledge."

"But how—?"

His question was cut off when he saw a small trail that led from the ledge upward, barely wide enough for two people. He froze in horror.

"Don't be afraid," the stranger comforted. Just trust me and let me do most of the work."

Slowly and carefully the two started up the path. It was narrow and the going was difficult, but they were able to make their way. "Now, here is where we may have a little problem."

He looked in front of him and saw that the path narrowed.

"Oh, that's just great," he said to himself. "I would be better off back on that ledge, waiting until some professional help came." He then remembered how close to death he was back there and how full of life he was now. "I'd best not complain."

The hermit moved out from under his arm. "Let me go first. You put your hands on my shoulders and walk in my footsteps. If you get tired or feel faint, tell me and we will stop. I'll be able to support you until you are ready to go again."

"I think I'll be able to do it. Let's go."

So they walked, the hermit in front and his charge behind him. Silently they inched their way up the trail.

His hands rested on the strong, broad shoulders of the hermit. At one point, he looked down at his feet and noticed for the first time that his rescuer was barefoot—and that his feet were bleeding. "It's no wonder," he thought, "these rocks are sharp. Why isn't he wearing anything on his feet?"

The trail abruptly leveled off and, looking around the one in front of him, he realized that they had reached the summit. About fifty yards away stood the ranger's cabin. Smoke curled from the chimney, signaling that the ranger was there.

"Here is where I must leave you," the stranger said. "Do you think that you can make it the rest of the way by yourself?"

He nodded, "I'm sure I can. But what can I say or do to thank you? You saved my life. I don't even know your name. Surely I can repay you in some way."

The hermit smiled. "No, there is nothing that is needed. I saved you because you needed to be saved. What I did had to be done. There is no question about that."

He took the hermit's hand in his and said, "Well, the very least I can say is thank you. Thank you very—" His hand felt damp. He looked down and saw that it was covered with blood, and in the stranger's hand—no in both of his hands—were deep wounds. And he saw that the blood on the trail did not come from cut feet but from wounds in his feet similar to those in his hands.

"How...? What...? Why...?" The question just wouldn't form. The hermit's smile was one of love and compassion. "Don't be concerned," he said. "It is the price I had to pay to save you."

Why do I do foolish things, Lord? I will take unnecessary risks with my life, but I am timid when it comes to serving you. Oh, I do not do dangerous things like climb mountains by myself. I just do things with my faith life that are not wise or prudent. And, when I fall? You are there. You always have been and I trust you always will be. I cannot doubt you. For when I have fallen the hardest or been in the most serious danger of losing my life, I have seen the print of the nails and know that I have been saved by the blood that was shed. But, the question remains: Why do I do foolish things? O Lord, I am confident that you will be there for me when I fall, for fall I will. Lead me along the path to salvation and do not abandon me. Amen.

Stuart's Hearing

Theme: grace
Scripture: 2 Kings 5:1-17; Luke 17:11-19
Season: Pentecost (21st Sunday, C cycle)

When the smoke cleared, Stuart and Lillian found themselves standing before a tribunal.

"Wha- What happened?" Stuart stammered.

"You had an accident."

Lillian snapped, "Well, I hope you are satisfied, Mr. Right-Of-Way. Now you've really done it, haven't you? If I've told you once, I've told you a thousand times that some time your need to have your way was going to get you into trouble. Well here you are and you had to bring me with you."

"But I had the right of way! What's the use of having laws if we aren't going to follow them? I can't help it if that knucklehead didn't know enough to yield. I was right."

"And look where being right got you. I don't see the other guy anywhere around here, do you?"

"I don't think all that bickering will be very helpful. We need to get on with the hearing." The voice came from a figure seated behind a raised desk. When they first looked, it seemed to be out of focus. But as they strained their eyes, the image became sharper and clearer. The person behind the desk was obviously a judge or the presider over the tribunal.

Stu and Lil couldn't believe what they saw. Lillian had to cover her mouth to keep from laughing out loud. The judge was dressed in the tradition of Old England with robe and wig. Only, half of the wig and the robe was white. The other half was black. Then to their astonishment they realized that the assembled tribunal reflected the same oddity. Half of them were dressed all in white, the other half in black.

A uniformed woman, who had been seated behind a desk, stood and said in a full and authoritative voice, "Oyez, Oyez, the hearing for Stuart Dillan is now in session, the honorable Lord presiding."

"Wait a minute. Wait just one darned minute here." Stuart was enraged. "I didn't hear Lillian's name mentioned."

"This isn't Lillian's hearing," responded His Honor.

"Aren't we both dead?"

"Who said anything about dead? I just said you had an accident. Now, let's get this show on the road. Mrs. Dillan, Lillian, would you please take the stand."

Lil entered the dock and sat on the chair.

"Now, Lillian," His Honor started, "I want you to tell us—"

"Uh, Your Honor," she interrupted, "aren't you going to swear me in?"

The judge looked directly at her. "No. I really wouldn't recommend anything but the truth here. Please tell us about Stu's understanding of right and wrong."

"Well, what is there to say? Things are either black or white for him." The tribunal started to shake their heads. "For Stuart, people get exactly what they deserve."

"Ooooooh" chorused the tribunal in unison and harmony.

"He is unbending in what he sees as right and wrong."

"Tsk, tsk," whispered the tribunal.

"Why, when he rents videos he will only bring home John Wayne movies because he says 'You can always tell the good guys from the bad guys.'"

The tribunal hooted and whistled.

His Honor glared at Stuart. "Is this correct?"

"Yeh. It is. So what? Things would be a lot more shipshape in life if more people felt the way I did."

The tribunal snickered.

The judge picked up a sheaf of papers from his desk and handed them to Stuart. "Here, read these."

Stuart took the papers. His eyes started to bulge as he read. "Where did you get these?"

"Oh, we have our own system here. What you are reading we call sins in these parts, and I call sin the leprosy of the soul. Now, Mr. People-Should-Get-What-They-Deserve, what do you have to say for yourself?"

"I'm dead meat!"

The tribunal cheered.

Stuart looked up at the judge and saw behind him a scene. It was the silhouette of a hill on which were three crosses.

"Stuart," the judge said, "I am going to pass the verdict. I am going to give you more than you deserve. I am going to forgive you."

The tribunal broke out in applause.

Stuart could not believe what he heard. This is not the way justice worked in his system. He was filled with a joy he had never felt before, and a warmth toward others. "Maybe I have to be more understanding toward others," he thought to himself. "I do need to be more careful with judgments I make."

Just then he felt a sharp pain in his ribs on the left side. The pain was caused by Lillian's elbow, which had just poked him. She leaned over and whispered, "Really, Stuart, you fell asleep during the sermon again. I don't know why you even bother coming to church. You never hear anything that is said."

Stuart smiled, "I wouldn't be too sure of that, Lil. I wouldn't be too sure."

Blessed and most patient God, I come to you as one who wants everything to be black and white and as one who wants all of the cards stacked in my favor. Many times I have insisted that I am right at the expense of the feelings and friendships of others. I have also made that error of using the words "all," "always," and "never" in such a way as to prevent others whom I deem less deserving to share in your glory. I thank you that my word is not the final authority and that in your own redeeming way you reveal the truth to me, a truth that at the same time judges and saves. Hear my fervent plea for your understanding and for time to amend my own sinful life. Send your Holy Spirit to guide, strengthen, and enlighten. Amen.

Season Index

Pentecost 3rd Sunday, B cycle	Trouble in Paradise
Pentecost 4th or 5th Sunday, A cycle	What the Disciples Heard
Pentecost 4th Sunday, C cycle	The Solo
Pentecost 8th Sunday, C cycle	What Is One to Do?
Pentecost 12th Sunday, C cycle	Grandma Richardson's Treasure
Pentecost 16th Sunday, A cycle	The Night *They* Were There
Pentecost 16th Sunday, C cycle	Sal's Tavern
Pentecost 20th Sunday, A cycle	Among the Pots and Pans
Pentecost 21st Sunday, C cycle	Stuart's Hearing
Pentecost 24th Sunday, C cycle	One Cold and Windy Day
Pentecost 27th Sunday, A cycle	The Judgment of the Village
Pentecost 23rd or 24th Sunday, A cycle	The Truck Stop
Christmas ABC cycles	How the Christmas Star Got Its Light
General	The Delegation
General	Dennis Meets St. Peter

Scripture Index

Scripture	Story
Genesis 3:9-15	Trouble in Paradise
Exodus 3:7-10	Reruns
Numbers 21:4-9	You Want It Made out of What?
Deuteronomy 4:32-34, 39-40, 8:2-3, 14-16	The Light in the Lantern
2 Kings 5:1-17	Stuart's Hearing
2 Samuel 11:26-12:10	The Solo
Isaiah 58:7-10	Can This Be Home?
Matthew 2:1-2	How the Christmas Star Got Its Light
Matthew 4:1-11	The Report
Matthew 9:13-15	The Delegation
Matthew 18:15-20	The Night *They* Were There
Matthew 21:33-43	Among the Pots and Pans
Matthew 22:24-40, 25:1-13	The Truck Stop
Matthew 25:31-46	The Judgment of the Village
Matthew 28:1-10	First Light
Mark 1:12-13	The Report
Mark 16:1-8	First Light

Theme Index

Theme	Story
Acceptance	The Judgment of the Village
Being yourself	Among the Pots and Pans
Christian love	The Solo
Christmas	How the Christmas Star Got Its Light
Church (nature of)	The Picnic
Coming of Christ	The Truck Stop
Compassion	Held in the Arms of Grace Reruns Trouble in Paradise
Doing the right thing	What Is One to Do?
Encountering the living Christ	One Cold and Windy Day Sal's Tavern
Enlightenment	What the Disciples Heard
Faith	The Solo Unless I See
Gifts	Among the Pots and Pans
God's kingdom (a banquet)	The Night *They* Were There
God's laughter	First Light
God's passion	Trouble in Paradise

MORE?
YOU WANT MORE JAMES L. HENDERSCHEDT?

Read the other books by this author.

THE TOPSY–TURVY KINGDOM:
More Stories for Your Faith Journey
Paperbound $7.95, 122 pages, 5 ½" x 8 ½"
ISBN 0-89390-177-6

Twenty-one stories of faith that turn the ordinary into the extraordinary. Find out why Carmen is glad she has to work on Thanksgiving Day, what happens when a busy man goes to a peace rally, and who was the greatest advance man any show ever had. In these stories bullies learn manners, workaholics find their way home, and young lawyers learn to use discernment with their clients. Through them all, the spiritual pilgrim will find deep, thought-provoking ideas. Use them for preaching, for religious education, or just for your own enjoyment.

THE MAGIC STONE
And Other Stories for the Faith Journey
Paperbound $7.95, 95 pages, 5 ½" x 8 ½"
ISBN 0-89390-116-4

The eternal wisdom of Scripture comes alive in the everyday setting of modern life in The Magic Stone. Read this book for enrichment, share the stories with others—your congregation, adult education class, or prayer group—and watch the word come to life for them. These inspirational stories are filled with touches of humor and suspense. Delightful, amazing, and most of all thought provoking, the reader or the listener will reflect on the real meaning behind the story and its spiritual significance for their own lives.

OTHER GOOD BOOKS ABOUT STORIES AND STORYTELLING

STORY AS A WAY TO GOD
A Guide for Storytellers
by H. Maxwell Butcher
Paperbound, $11.95 153 pages, 5 ½" x 8 ½"
ISBN: 0- 89390-201-2

This book will open your eyes to find God's story everywhere. The message of God is hidden in our novels, movies, poems, and plays. The homilist, the teacher, and the counselor will learn how to improve their storytelling skills as they read Maxwell Butcher's careful analysis of story type from comedy and tragedy to melodrama and "resurrection literature." Tips include how to avoid a "too easy" ending, and why a story must "stretch" the reader. From Sound of Music to Lord of the Rings the author convinces you that telling a story is the best way to share the Christian message, and he challenges you to be open to ways that you, too, can tell God's story.

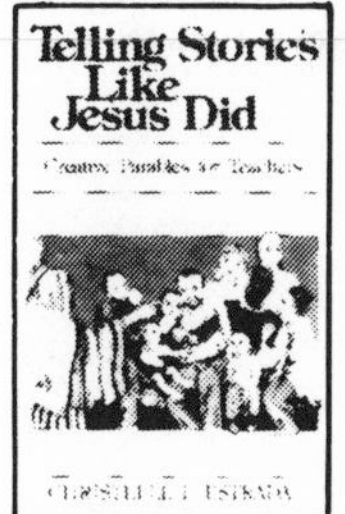

TELLING STORIES LIKE JESUS DID
Creative Parables for Teachers
by Christelle L. Estrada
Paperbound $8.95, 100 pages, 5 ½" x 8 ½"
ISBN 0-89390-177-6

Christelle Estrada retells ten parables from Luke's Gospel and after each parable, she reinterprets its message in terms today's children can understand. Teachers who are searching for a way to interpret the Gospel message of salvation for today's children will find this book an excellent guide. The author says that the word "Salvation" originally meant "health and wholeness," and choosing to follow it is a move toward wholeness for a broken world. These stories will give you insight on how to interpret other Gospel stories, and they will make you pause and think about how you apply the Gospel in your own life.

FORGIVE
Stories of Reconciliation
by Lou Ruoff
Paperbound, $8.95, 102 pages, 5 ½" x 8 ½"
ISBN 0-89390-198-9

In falling autumn leaves, Lou Ruoff sees the power of fallen humans to heal themselves and others; in the tears of a little girl he sees the hope that Judas lacked; in a simple request for eye glasses he sees the answer to humanity's distorted vision. The author combines stories from the Bible with his own experience of hurt, rejection, discrimination, and anger. In the power and simplicity of his stories, Ruoff draws the reader to trust in God's love to forgive and be forgiven. The message of these stories will stay with you for a long time.

STORYTELLING STEP BY STEP
by Marsh Cassady
Paperbound, $9.95, 156 pages, 5 ½" x 8 ½"
ISBN 0-89390-183-0

This is the basic handbook for storytellers. Marsh Cassady carefully breaks down the elements needed for successful storytelling. Find out about the relationship between the story and the teller. Learn how to adapt a story for a particular audience and how to hold that audience's attention; how to choose a story that matches the occasion, and how to use voice, gesture and props to enhance your storytelling. The author, a director, editor, and free-lance writer, puts his teaching into action in the book's stories.

CREATING STORIES FOR STORYTELLING
by Marsh Cassady
Paperbound, $9.95 144 pages, 5 ½" x 8 ½"
ISBN 0-89390-205-5

Cassady continues to instruct his readers in the art of storytelling in this new book. Here he gives tips on how to get ideas for creating your own stories, how to develop a plot, create tension, and write dialogue that will hold your listener's attention.

NO KIDDING, GOD, WHERE ARE YOU?
by Lou Ruoff
Parables of Ordinary Experience
Paperbound, $7.95 100 pages, 5 ½" x 8 ½"
ISBN 0-89390-141-5

Feeling alone? Abandoned by God? Read these extraordinary stories of the ordinary and the Gospel message will come alive to you in a new and deeper way. Lou Ruoff, with his keen perception of the average person's pain, uses his wonderful storytelling gifts to apply the lessons in Jesus' parables to the commonplace happenings of modern life. Find the message in a smashed sand castle at the beach, and see the love of God in a game of hopscotch. This book is loaded with spiritual nourishment for everyone.

WINTER DREAMS: and Other Such Friendly Dragons
by Joseph J. Juknialis
Paperbound $7.95, 87 pages, 6" x 9"
ISBN 0-89390-010-9

Delightful, gentle stories that transport the reader to a world of hope. In drama, fairytale, and fable the author fills us with stories of old and valued principles. If Winter prepares us for birth, dreams prepare us for what will be. In these fifteen stories, let yourself rejoice that you live in the season of Winter and you journey through the dreams of your spirit.

BALLOONS! CANDY! TOYS!
And Other Parables for Storytellers
by Daryl Olszewski
Paperbound $8.95, 100 pages, 5 ½" x 8 ½"
ISBN 0-89390-069-9

Don't let the title fool you. This is no lightweight book of frothy stories for little kids. Daryl Olszewski's prayerful interpretations of nine parables from Scripture catch at the heart of the reader. He begins by reflecting on some aspect of a Gospel story like the heart of stone. Then he tells the story through the perception of an inanimate object and finishes with a commentary that shows how to make stories into faith experience for children and adults. This is great for teachers, storytellers, and anyone who enjoys new reflections on ageless Gospel stories.

ANGELS TO WISH BY: A Book of Story-Prayers
by Joseph Juknialis
Paperbound $7.95, 136 pages, 6" x 9"
ISBN 089390-051-6

These are beautiful stories that can be used in liturgical and paraliturgical celebrations. The book contains prayers, Scripture, reflections all pointed to giving the reader a deeper insight into Christian faith and what that faith calls us to do. Read about the Bag Lady, Josh and the free wish, the Banjo man. Sing the songs that accompany some of the stories. This book is a wonderful aid for teachers, homilists, and catechists.

A STILLNESS WITHOUT SHADOWS
by Joseph J. Juknialis
Paperbound $7.95 75 pages, 6" x 9"
ISBN 0-89390-081-8

If you enjoyed Joseph Juknialis other books, you will love A Stillness Without Shadows. These new stories spell out the way faith can be lived—but sometimes isn't. Read "The Lady of the Grand," "The Cup," or "The Golden Dove" to reflect on the depth of God's love and the strength of human weakness. Included is an appendix that gives wonderful tips on how to use the stories in liturgies and class settings.

WHEN GOD BEGAN IN THE MIDDLE
by Joseph J. Juknialis
Paperback $7.95, 101 pages, 6" x 9"
ISBN 0-89390-027-3

Our God is a God who comes into the middle of everything. God comes into the middle of our sin, and we begin to know mercy. He comes into the middle of our loneliness, and we begin to be transformed into the image and likeness of love. God comes into the middle of death, and gives life. Read these fantasy stories and reflect on times in your own life when God began in the middle.

STORIES FOR CHILDREN

PARABLES FOR LITTLE PEOPLE
by Lawrence Castagnola, S.J.
Paperbound $7.95, 101 pages, 5 ½" x 8 ½"
ISBN 0-89390-034-6

Sweet, humorous stories that teach children basic values. They will learn about race relations through "The Rainbow People," and overcoming self-pity through "Arnold the Elephant." Children will love these stories and ask for more, and teachers, catechists, and parents will delight in teaching children through these sixteen mighty little parables.

MORE PARABLES FOR LITTLE PEOPLE
by Larry Castagnola, S.J.
Paperbound 100 pages, 5 ½" x 8 ½"
ISBN 0-89390-095-8

This sequel to Parables for Little People has 15 more charming children's stories with happy, positive messages. Seven of the new stories teach the Gospel themes of sharing, caring, non-violence, and human rights. The rest retell the Gospel stories without naming the original characters. This is a great book for children, teachers, and parents.

ORDER FORM

Order from your local religious bookstore, or mail this form to:

QTY	TITLE	PRICE	TOTAL

Subtotal:________

CA residents add 7¼% sales tax:________

(Santa Clara Co. add 8¼% sales tax)

*Postage and handling:________

Total amount:________

*Postage and handling
$2.00 for orders up to $20.00
10% of orders over $20.00 but less than $150.00
$15.00 for order of $150.00 or more

RESOURCE
Resource Publications, Inc.
160 E. Virginia St., Suite 290
San Jose, CA 95112-5876
or call (408) 286-8505

☐ My check or money order is enclosed.

☐ Charge my ❑ VISA ❑ MC Exp. date:________

Card#________-________-________-________

Signature:________________________

Name:________________________

Institution: ________________________

Street:________________________

City/St/Zip: ________________________